Amazing
BEN FRANKLIN
Inventions
You Can Build Yourself

Carmella Van Vleet

nomad press

Nomad Press

A division of Nomad Communications

10 9 8 7 6 5 4 3 2 1

Softcover ISBN 13: 9780977129478

Hardcover ISBN 13: 9780979226885

Questions regarding the ordering of this book should be addressed to

Independent Publishers Group

814 N. Franklin St., Chicago, IL 60610

www.ipgbook.com

Nomad Press

2456 Christian St., White River Junction, VT 05001

www.nomadpress.net

Other titles from Nomad Press

Praise for Carmella Van Vleet's
Great Ancient Egypt Projects You Can Build Yourself

"This truly fascinating book makes connections to history, math, and science while focusing mainly on the art and culture of ancient Egypt."
—School Arts Magazine, April 2007

"A wealth of interesting information and clever hands-on projects… Many of the projects could help teachers fulfill curriculum objectives."
—Children's Literature

"The ideas will be useful for school projects or individual crafting fun. This title will be a useful and popular addition to any collection…"
—School Library Journal, February 2007

Praise for Carmella Van Vleet's
How to Handle School Snafus

"Former elementary school teacher Van Vleet offers parents simple remedies to the most common [school related] problems. Her book reads quickly, and her suggestions make sense."
—School Library Journal

"A quick-hit answer for many school crises."
—Kansas City Star

"A very readable book. Should be on the shelves of every household with elementary school kids. A great blend of humor and practical wisdom."
—Trevor Romain, author of *"Bullies Are a Pain in the Brain"*

"From general information to specific answers to parents' concerns, this handbook is an invaluable resource for any parent with school-aged children. Topics are easy to access and answers to questions are cross-referenced for ease of use. A must in every parent involvement library."
—Lynn Salem and Josie Stewart, Seedling Publications

Contents

Ben Franklin: A Timeline

1706 Born on January 17 in Boston, Massachusetts

1716 Invents swim fins

1718 Begins apprenticeship with his brother, James, in James' printing shop

1723 Runs away to Philadelphia, Pennsylvania

1724 Sails to London where he becomes a master printer

1728 Opens a printing office in Philadelphia

1729 Becomes sole owner and publisher of *The Pennsylvania Gazette*

1731 Founds the first public library in America

1732 Begins publishing *Poor Richard's Almanac*

1736 Founds the first fire company in America

1737 Appointed Postmaster of Philadelphia

1742 Proposes the idea for the University of Pennsylvania; invents Pennsylvania Fireplace

1748 Retires from printing and business and begins experimenting with electricity

1752 Performs his famous kite experiment

1757 Goes to England as a Colonial Representative

1769 Elected president of the American Philosophical Society

1775 Elected to the Continental Congress

1776 Signs the Declaration of Independence; sails to France as American Commissioner

1778 Negotiates and signs Treaty of Alliance with France

1779 Appointed Minister to France

1782 Negotiates the Treaty of Peace with Great Britain

1784 Invents bifocals

1785 Returns to Philadelphia

1786 Publishes map of the Gulf Stream

1787 Elected president of the Pennsylvania Society for Promoting the Abolition of Slavery; serves as delegate to the Constitutional Convention

1790 Dies on April 17 at age 84 in Philadelphia

Introduction

ave you ever seen a lightning rod on top of a skyscraper or known someone who wore bifocals? Have you ever visited a fire station or checked out a book at a public library? Have you ever used paper money to buy something? Or learned about the Declaration of Independence or the Constitution of the United States? All these things have something in common—Benjamin Franklin either invented them or contributed to their creation in a major way.

Ben Franklin was an amazing man, and he led an amazing life. He was an important inventor, a highly successful writer and printer, a well-respected scientist, and a clever politician who helped found America. He lived for 84 years and accomplished so many

Ben Franklin

things that it would be nearly impossible to talk about them all. But this book will at least give you a good picture of Ben's most significant inventions and contributions to society. You'll discover things like how Ben's childhood love of water led to the invention of swimming paddles, how his love of music led to the invention of the **armonica**, and how his natural curiosity led to very important discoveries about electricity. You'll see how Ben's writing changed people's lives and shaped a country. Along the way, you'll also learn about Ben himself, as well as his friends and family.

Most of the projects in this book can be made with supplies you probably have at home or that you can easily find at a craft or hardware store, and they can be done without too much adult supervision. So step back into colonial America, and get ready to Build it Yourself!

An armonica.

Words to Know

armonica: a musical instrument of the eighteenth and nineteenth centuries made out of hemispherical glasses that turn on an axis and are played by touching the edges with a dampened finger. Hemispherical means half of a globe, like the shape of a bowl.

Swim Paddles

Benjamin Franklin grew up along the Charles River in Boston, Massachusetts. Like many kids who lived in the American **colonies** in the early 1700s, Ben loved to play outdoors.

He also loved the water. Ben liked to boat and canoe with his friends, and he loved to swim. He taught himself how to swim when he was eight, and he often taught his friends how to swim as well. In fact, when Ben was older and living in England, someone suggested that he open up a school to teach swimming. Ben considered the idea, but then decided to stick with his plan of returning to America to start a **print shop**.

Ben swimming.

Children in colonial times played many games that children today play. For instance, Ben and his friends probably enjoyed things such as swinging on swings and playing leapfrog and hopscotch, as well as games with playing cards, pick-up sticks, and the string game known as cat's cradle. Colonial children also played with homemade toys like cornhusk dolls, yo-yos, and spinning toys called whirligigs.

Colonial Toys & Games

Even at a young age, Ben was a good observer and inventor. When he was swimming, he saw that some kids could swim faster than others. Ben decided to experiment with ways to make himself go faster both on the surface and under the water. He believed that the size of a swimmer's hands and feet might be the difference, so when he was around 10 years old, he invented swim paddles. His hand paddles were made of oval-shaped pieces of wood. They had holes cut out for his thumbs and straps that went over the rest of his fingers. Ben also made flippers for his feet. Ben described these flippers as "a kind of sandals" that he fitted to the soles of his feet. The swim paddles and flippers worked great, just the way Ben had hoped they would!

Young Ben thought of another way to make himself move faster in the water. This time, he used a kite. As the story goes, he and a friend were out flying kites one day when Ben went down to the water

Ben was born on a Sunday, which was considered bad luck during the eighteenth century. He was also left-handed. This, too, was considered bad luck.

and laid on his back in it. He held onto the kite string and let the kite pull him around. As an older man, in a letter to a friend, he described the experience this way: "I began to cross the pond with my kite, which carried me quite over

Ben Franklin being pulled by a kite.

without the least fatigue and with the greatest pleasure imaginable."

Later in life, Ben would be considered a great leader. But Ben started showing his leadership skills as a child. Unfortunately, he was sometimes mischievous and got himself and his friends in trouble. For example, one time Ben organized a group of friends to carry stones and build a **wharf** for an area of the pond they played near. The project was hard work and took an entire evening. The problem was that the stones they used were taken from a house construction site! The next morning, when the construction workers made

Words to Know

colonies: groups of British settlements in America.

print shop: a place where books, newspapers and other items are printed.

wharf: a dock or platform built from the shore out over water.

autobiography: a book a person writes about his or her life.

Julian calendar: a calendar introduced in Rome in 46 BCE.

The 12-month year has 365 days except each fourth year has 366 days.

Each month has 31 or 30 days, except February—which has 28 or in leap years 29 days.

Gregorian calendar: a calendar introduced in 1582 by Pope Gregory XIII to revise the Julian calendar to bring it back into synchronization with the seasons. It was adopted in Great Britain and the American colonies in 1752. The Gregorian calendar does not add the extra day to February in a century year unles it is divisible by four.

Ben was the 15th kid in a family of 17 kids! He was born on January 6, 1706, but many resources record his birth date as January 17. This is because America used the Julian calendar at the time Ben was born. In 1752 America and other British territories began using the Gregorian calendar. In the process of changing over, 11 days were lost—and New Year's Day moved from March to January!

Ben and his friends put the stones all back, Ben's dad, Josiah, was unhappy with Ben. Even though Ben tried to argue that the wharf was useful, Josiah was not impressed. In his **autobiography**, Ben wrote about the event. He recalled that his dad, "convinced me that nothing was useful which was not honest."

Colonial children typically had many siblings.

Throughout his life, Ben was a great believer in exercise. He swam and lifted dumbbells into his eighties. Ben noticed his body temperature and heart rate went up when he exercised. And he suspected those things could help prevent diseases and illness. Today, of course, we know he was right and that regular exercise is good for our bodies.

Colonial families were often large. Families needed to have lots of children because they helped a lot with the family business or farm. It was common for children to die at a young age due to accident or illness. As a result, children in colonial times typically had plenty of brothers or sisters as well as neighborhood kids to play with.

Antique dumbbells.

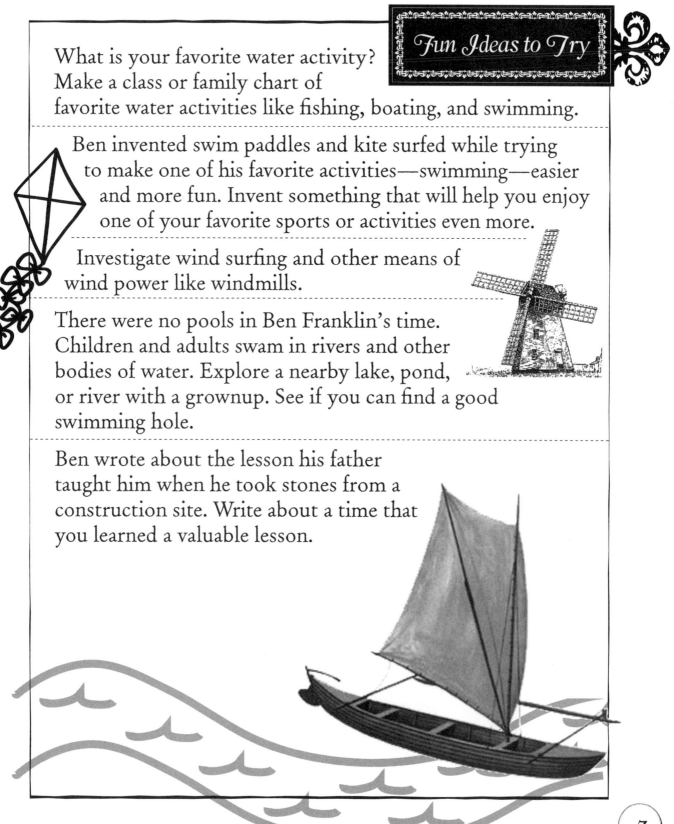

Fun Ideas to Try

What is your favorite water activity? Make a class or family chart of favorite water activities like fishing, boating, and swimming.

Ben invented swim paddles and kite surfed while trying to make one of his favorite activities—swimming—easier and more fun. Invent something that will help you enjoy one of your favorite sports or activities even more.

Investigate wind surfing and other means of wind power like windmills.

There were no pools in Ben Franklin's time. Children and adults swam in rivers and other bodies of water. Explore a nearby lake, pond, or river with a grownup. See if you can find a good swimming hole.

Ben wrote about the lesson his father taught him when he took stones from a construction site. Write about a time that you learned a valuable lesson.

Make Your Own
Swim Paddles

1 Lay the two lids down on your work surface. It doesn't matter which side is facing up; the paddles will work in the water either way. It's more comfortable for your hands, though, if the side with writing (or where the label was) is facing up.

2 Start with one lid. Imagine your lid is the face of a clock. Find where "7 o'clock" is and mark it with the pen. Poke a hole through the mark with the pointy scissors. Afterwards, lift up the lid and carefully use the scissors to cut a hole about the size of a quarter around the mark, near the edge of the lid. (Make sure there is an adult around while you use the pointy scissors!) This is your thumbhole and this paddle will be for your right hand.

3 Place your right thumb into the hole. Relax the rest of your fingers so that they lay flat against the lid. Don't spread your fingers out too wide or hold them too close together. Use the pen to make dots to the right of the middle knuckle of your pointer

Supplies

* **2 round plastic lids***
* **protection for your work surface, such as a piece of cardboard, cutting board, or a magazine**
* **pointy scissors**
* **2 shoelaces, any color***
* **permanent markers, any color**
* **spray paint, any color (optional)**

*Lids from 12 ounce plastic food containers work well. If the lid is too much bigger than your hands, the paddles will not move through the water easily. Make sure they are clean and dry. Shoelaces should be the kind for athletic shoes, not dress shoes. The laces don't need to be long.

finger and to the left of the middle knuckle of your pinky.

4 Lay the lid back down on your protective surface. Use the scissors to poke holes through the marks. Next, poke one shoelace end into one of the holes and tie a knot at the end of the lace. The knot should be on the front of the paddle. (The back of the paddle is where the palms of your hands will rest.)

5 Poke the other end of the lace into the other lid hole. This should form a strap for your fingers. Pull the lace snug and tie a knot at the end. Cut off any extra lace. It's easier to get the strap the right length if you ask someone else to pull the lace and make the second knot.

6 To make a paddle for your left hand, make a

mark and cut a thumbhole in your second lid at "5 o'clock." Next, follow the same steps you used to make your right-hand paddle.

7 If you want, spray paint your paddles following the directions on the paint can and let them dry. Note that the paint will eventually wear off in the water. Another option is to use permanent markers to decorate your paddles. Now you're ready to try out your swim paddles in the water!

Time needed:

15 minutes, not including drying time for paint

Pennsylvania Fireplace

Ben started inventing things as a young boy, but he came up with many of his well-known inventions later on in life, between the ages of 40 and 49.

By this time, Ben had already lived a good and full life—and yet he still had well over 30 more years to enjoy! Ben was happily married to a woman named Deborah Read. They were raising Ben's son, William, and their daughter Sarah, who they nicknamed Sally. Another son of theirs, Francis, had became ill and died when he was just four years old.

Deborah, above, and Sarah, below.

There is a famous story about the first time Deborah Read saw Ben Franklin. Ben, who was just 17, had recently sailed to Philadelphia from New York, where he'd run away after a big fight with his brother. Ben was exhausted and tired from the boat ride, which took much longer than expected because of a storm, and from walking for two days to catch another boat to take him to Philadelphia. Ben was nearly out of money and very hungry. With his pockets stuffed with what little clothes he had, he went to a nearby bakery. There, he spent three pennies on what Ben described in his autobiography as "great puffy rolls." He carried one roll in each of his hands and, having no more room in his pockets, put the other two under each arm. Next, he set off down Market Street. This is where Deborah, standing in her doorway, saw him. She thought he looked funny and laughed. Later on (in his autobiography) Ben agreed that he made a ". . . most awkward, ridiculous appearance."

By the halfway point of Ben's life, he had established himself as a **printer** and author and was turning his attention to other things, including inventing. In 1742, Ben invented a stove. Before Franklin's stove, fires in fireplaces heated colonial homes, which wasn't very safe. Most colonial houses were made of wood, and so one spark from a fireplace could lead to a fire that destroyed a home quickly. On top of that, heating a home with a fireplace didn't work too well. Much of the heat

Deborah was the daughter of Ben's landlady.

Pennsylvania Fireplace.

was lost as it went right up the chimney into the sky.

Because Ben had done some experiments with heat and air, he knew how they circulated. He used this knowledge to design an iron "box" that fit inside most fireplaces. This open stove used a series of metal chambers to warm air and direct it out through side panels. Ben called his stove a **Pennsylvania Fireplace** and, in 1744, he wrote a **pamphlet** that described and praised the invention. The pamphlet claimed the stove was safer to use than an open fire, helped reduce cold drafts (and therefore prevented illnesses according to Ben), and used less wood than a traditional fireplace because the wood burned longer. All this was true, and Ben knew it—but it

No one knows who William's mother was. All we know is that Ben was given full responsibility to raise the boy.

Color & Heat Absorption

One sunny, winter morning, Ben did an interesting experiment with heat. He wanted to see if certain colors got hot faster than other colors. In a letter he wrote to a pen pal, Ben described how he took a number of little pieces of cloth of all shades of colors and laid them out on the snow. Next, he waited for several hours. When he returned, Ben found the black and dark blue pieces of cloth had sunk the lowest. The lighter colors had sunk in the snow very little. And the white piece of cloth was still on top of the snow. From this, Ben reasoned that dark colors absorb heat. In his letter, Ben wrote that we could learn from his experiment "that black clothes are not so fit to wear in a hot sunny climate or season as white ones."

Ben and Deborah had a common law marriage. This is where two people live together as a couple but aren't officially married. Ben and Deborah couldn't legally marry because Deborah's first husband ran off and no one could prove he was dead. It was against the law for Deborah to remarry if her first husband might be alive.

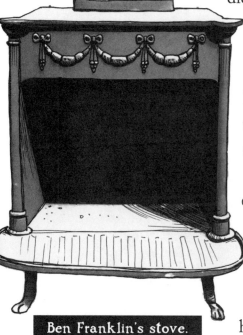

Ben Franklin's stove.

did have a big design flaw. Since it had no fresh air circulating through it the fire went out quickly and smoke came out a hole in the bottom of the stove. Eventually, another Philadelphia inventor named David Rittenhouse designed an "L" shaped chimney that fixed this problem. After the improvement, the stove became very popular.

Ben was offered a **patent** on the stove. A patent is a document that says a person owns an invention so no one else can make it or sell it. Even though this would have made Ben lots of money he didn't patent the stove—or anything else he invented for that matter. He said, "As we enjoy great advantages from the inventions of others, we should be glad of an opportunity to serve others by any invention of ours; and this we should do freely and generously."

Words to Know

printer: someone who prints words on paper and sells them for a living.

Pennsylvania Fireplace: the stove Ben Franklin invented that was inserted into chimneys.

pamphlet: a short book or brochure that describes something.

patent: a document that says a person owns an invention so no one else can get official credit for it or make it or sell it.

Make Your Own
Solar-Powered Oven

Ben Franklin invented a stove that helped heat colonial homes during cold winters. This solar oven won't produce enough heat to warm a house, but it will generate enough heat to cook food!

1 Draw a square on the closed pizza box's lid. The square should be about an inch smaller than the lid.

2 Use the scissors to cut the square on three sides. Don't cut the side along the back of the box. Fold along the uncut edge to make a flap.

3 Open the flap and cover the inside of it with a piece of aluminum foil, shiny side out. Smooth the foil as best you can and tape it or glue it (with non-toxic glue) down. This foil-covered flap is your solar reflector.

4 Use more foil, shiny side out, to line the inside bottom and sides of the pizza box.

5 Lay the construction paper on the inside bottom of the pizza box. It should cover the bottom of the box completely. Tape it down.

Supplies

* 1 pizza box
* marker
* scissors
* aluminum foil
* tape or non-toxic glue (do not use duct tape as it will give off toxic fumes)
* black construction paper
* clear plastic wrap (oven cooking bags or plastic window wrap will work too)
* a wooden dowel about 10 inches long

6 Open the pizza lid. Cut a piece of clear plastic to fit over the opening you made when you made the flap. The plastic should be bigger than the flap (reflector) opening. Tape it down and make sure there are no gaps for heat to escape.

7 Close the lid and prop open the solar reflector (the flap) with the dowel. Now, you're ready to start cooking!

Time needed:
45 minutes, not including cooking time

Ben said "To lengthen thy life, lessen thy meals."

To cook with your solar oven:

1 Place your oven on a flat, outdoor surface in direct sunlight. Adjust the reflector so it directs the maximum amount of sunlight into the oven.

2 Use the dowel to hold up the reflector. If the dowel is too long or won't stay in place, try using a drinking straw.

3 For best results, keep adjusting your oven and reflector as the sun moves throughout the day. Note that the best time of day to use your oven is between 9 a.m. and 3 p.m. Preheat your oven for about 30 minutes.

4 After preheating, open the lid and place your food inside. You can put your food on a napkin or paper plate or on a piece of foil. Close the lid and that's it!

5 Depending on what you're cooking and how warm the day is, cooking times will vary. You should count on it taking at least an hour or more to cook your food. Try to resist the temptation to keep opening the lid to check. Every time you open the lid, the oven loses heat.

Fun Ideas to Try

Re-create Ben's colored-cloth experiment. No snow? Try using crushed ice.

Deborah Read's first impression of Ben Franklin wasn't great. In spite of that, she fell in love with him and married him. Share a time when your first impression of someone turned out to be wrong.

Draw a funny picture of Ben strolling into Philadelphia with all those rolls under his arms.

Ben wrote a pamphlet about his stove. Write a pamphlet describing the benefits of a new invention or describing how to put it together and use it.

Re-read what Ben said about serving others by giving inventions freely. Debate whether Ben should have patented his inventions. Discuss what would happen if no scientists and inventors patented their work. Would there be any downside to this?

Put an oven thermometer inside your solar oven and keep track of the temperature throughout the day. How does cloud cover affect the temperature?

Make Your Own
Baked Apple

Because they grew so well in northern states, apples were popular in colonial times. Here's an easy recipe for a solar-baked apple using your solar oven.

1 Arrange your apple slices on the paper plate. Sprinkle the brown sugar, raisins, and cinnamon on top. You can use as much or as little cinnamon as you'd like.

2 Place the apples inside your solar oven and bake for 1 to 2 hours or until the apple slices are soft. Then, enjoy!

Here are a few more food ideas to try in your solar oven: hotdogs, English muffin pizzas, s'mores, biscuits, cheese sandwiches, steamed vegetables (make a foil bowl and add a tiny bit of water), brownies (put mix in a foil baking cup that's been cut in half). Note: before you eat anything you cook in your oven, have your parents check and make sure it is completely cooked.

Supplies

* ✳ 1 large apple, sliced in circles or wedges
* ✳ 1 tablespoon brown sugar
* ✳ snack-sized box of raisins
* ✳ cinnamon
* ✳ paper plate

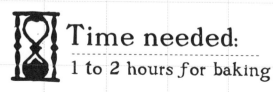

Time needed:
1 to 2 hours for baking

Armonica

Ben loved many things: experimenting, reading, writing, and helping his city and country. He also loved music. He loved listening to it, and he loved playing it. It was his love of music that inspired him to invent his very own instrument: the armonica.

In 1757, Ben left Philadelphia for England. He did so because the **Pennsylvania Assembly** had asked him to serve as its agent. The Penn family, which ruled the colony, did not pay taxes on its land to support Pennsylvania, which the Assembly thought was unfair. Ben accepted the job, and, after crossing the Atlantic with his son William, moved into a house in London. No one knew for certain how long Ben would be there, not even Ben himself. It turned out to be five years!

William Penn

Ben called music "the most pleasing science."

While in England, Ben had an active social life. He had many, many friends and regularly discussed science and other interesting things with some of England's greatest thinkers. For example, one of Ben's friends was Joseph Priestley. Mr. Priestley was a **pastor** turned chemist who, among other things, discovered that plants take in carbon dioxide and give off oxygen. He also invented soda water and rubber erasers! Ben also went out often. It was during one of these outings that Ben attended a concert where the musician played songs by rubbing his fingers along the rims of glasses filled with various amounts of water.

Ben loved the eerie, beautiful music, but he thought running fingers around the rims of glasses was too much work. He set out to make the process easier. First, he asked a glass blower named Charles James to make 37 crystal bowls in various sizes and widths. At Ben's request, the bottom of each bowl had a hole in the center. Next, Ben turned the bowls on their sides, arranged them from largest to smallest, and ran an iron rod through the holes in the bottom of each bowl. Cork kept the bowls from banging into each other and from banging against the iron rod. He then set the bowls in a shallow pan of water and attached the rod to a belt turned by a foot pedal. This way the bowls turned, and all the musician had to do was move his fingers around to play the

Ben Franklin was the first American to invent an instrument.

An armonica.

The armonica was very popular, especially in Europe. Marie Antoinette, Queen of France, even took armonica lessons.

Ben and his daughter Sally playing a duet.

notes he wanted. Ben made playing notes even easier by painting the bowl rims black, white, and the colors of the rainbow. The new instrument was named the armonica after the Italian word *armonia*, which means "harmony." Over the years the instrument has also been called the glass armonica and the glass harmonica, which is kind of surprising since the *harmonica* is a wind instrument!

Because musicians could play more than one note at a time, they could make more complicated music on the armonica than on plain old glasses. The instrument had a lovely, almost haunting, quality that inspired many famous composers to write music for it—including Wolfgang Amadeus Mozart and Ludwig van Beethoven. In fact, the armonica had such an unusual and "heavenly" sound it got Ben in a bit of trouble one night. As the story goes, Ben was playing the armonica late one night and woke up Deborah. Hearing the eerie soft notes, she was sure she had died and gone to heaven!

Of all his inventions, Ben considered the armonica his personal favorite. Along with playing other instruments such as the harp, guitar, and violin, Ben played his armonica throughout his life. Often, he played **duets** with his daughter Sally. The two of them spent many hours in the music room of their Philadelphia home. This third-floor room was known as the Blue Room. (Yes. It was painted blue!)

Words to Know

Pennsylvania Assembly: the colonial government in Pennsylvania.
pastor: a leader of a Christian group or church, especially one which is Protestant.
duet: a song played or sung by two performers.

While he was in England, Ben's son, William, went to school and earned a law degree in 1758. Right before he and his father returned to America, William married Elizabeth Downes and was appointed governor of the New Jersey colony.

Fun Ideas to Try

In a letter to a friend, Ben described how he was inspired by a musician playing music on wine glasses. He wrote, "Being charmed by the sweetness of its tones, and the music he produced from it, I wished only to see the glasses disposed in a more convenient way . . ." Write your own letter to a friend describing how you would improve an existing musical instrument.

Listen to what an armonica sounds like at: http://sln.fi.edu/franklin/musician/virtualarmonica.html.

Ben planned a special room for music for his house in Philadelphia. Design your own music room.

Read about the history of other instruments.

When he was seven years old, Ben was so delighted by the sound of a whistle that he bought it from the owner for four times its worth! Ben's siblings teased him, but he learned a valuable lifelong lesson about being careful with your money.

Tabletop Music Stand

Making an armonica would require help from a glass blower. You can recreate the sound, though. All you need to do is fill a wine glass about a quarter to a half full of water. Wine glasses work best, but be sure to ask your parent's permission first! Next, dip your finger in the water and then gently move it around the rim of the glass. Keep moving your finger until you hear a "ring." Fill several glasses with various amounts of water to produce more notes. Now, you can compose your own music! To hold your music, here is a tabletop music stand you can make.

1 Lay your foam board (or layers of cardboard) on the cutting board and, using the knife, cut a 12-by-12 inch square. Then cut two strips that are 12 inches long and 1 inch wide.

2 Carefully cut one of the strips in half, lengthwise. This will give you two strips that are 12 inches long and a half-inch wide. Glue the long sides of these pieces together to form an "L" shape. Set the piece aside to allow the glue to dry. This will be part of the tray for your music stand later on.

Supplies

* large piece of foam board (or layers of thick cardboard)

* cutting board

* ruler

* utility knife (Be sure to get an adult's permission and help with this tool!)

* craft glue

* white duct tape or clear strapping tape (masking tape will work in a pinch but it doesn't hold up as well)

* piece of ribbon, any color or width, about 8 inches long

* markers

3 The 12-by-1-inch strip will be the "foot" that holds up your music stand. To attach the foot, first lay the square flat. Find the middle of one side. Lay the strip perpendicular to the square at that middle point. Then, use a piece of tape to attach the two pieces. Turn the two pieces over. Fold them together. Put another piece of tape over the fold.

4 Adjust the foot so your music stand is an angle you like. A 45-degree angle works well. Cut your ribbon to fit in between the foot and the back of the music stand and attach one end of the ribbon to the foot and the other end to the back of the stand. You can use glue or tape. This ribbon will keep your music tray from sliding flat.

5 Finally, glue the long "L"-shaped piece along the bottom front of the music stand. Now, you have a tray to hold up your music. If your music needs more support, you can use a clothes pin to clip to the back of the stand.

6 Decorate your tabletop music stand with the markers, and you're ready to start composing music or writing lyrics!

Time needed:
45 minutes

My Plain Country Joan

Ben wrote a song for his wife, Deborah, called "My Plain Country Joan." Joan was a name that meant any woman. Here are the lyrics:

Of all the Chloes and Philisses Poets may prate
I sing my plain Country Joan
Now twelve years my wife, Still the joy of my life,
Bless'd day that I made her my own.

Not a word of her face, her shape, or her eyes,
Of flames or of darts shall you hear,
Tho' I beauty admire, 'tis virtue I prize,
That fades not in seventy years.

In health a companion, delightful and dear,
Still easy, engaging and free,
In sickness no less than the faithfullest nurse
As tender as tender can be.

In peace and good order my household she keeps
Right careful to save what I gain
Yet cheerfully spends and smiles on the friends
I've the pleasure to entertain.

Am I laden with care, she takes off a large share,
That the burden never makes me to reel
Does good fortune arrive, the joy of my wife
Quite doubles the pleasure I feel.

Were the fairest young princess, with millions
in purse
To be had in exchange for my Joan,
She could not be a better wife, might be a worse,
So I'll cling to my lovely old Joan!

Bifocals, the Long Arm, and The Library Company of Philadelphia

When Ben was eight years old, his father, Josiah, sent him to the Boston Latin School. Josiah wanted to prepare Ben for Harvard, where he hoped Ben would eventually study to become a minister.

Ben did very well at Boston Latin. He even quickly jumped ahead a grade. But because of the high cost, Josiah took Ben out of the school after only one year. The next year, Josiah enrolled Ben at a neighborhood academy called Brownell's School for Writing and Arithmetic. There, Ben did very well in writing but he failed at math.

Ben left his second school after only one year as well. But he carried his love of reading and writing throughout his life. In his autobiography, Ben wrote: "From a child, I was fond of reading, and all the little money that came into my hands was ever laid out in books." Later on, when Ben

Colonial Schools

Colonial schools were not like schools today. They were usually small, one-room houses, and instructors could be quite strict. Students might be whipped for misbehaving. Girls and boys learned things like Latin, math, and writing. Many students used a **hornbook** or a copy of the New England Primer to learn to read. A hornbook was not really a book with pages; it was a paddle-shaped piece of wood with one piece of paper glued to the top. This paper had the alphabet and a bible verse, usually The Lord's Prayer, on it. Hornbooks got their name from the thin piece of cow horn that covered the piece of paper. This see-through material was used to protect the paper, which was expensive. The New England Primer was a 90-page book that also contained the alphabet and bible verses. It also had abbreviations and rhymes to help students learn letters and lessons.

was an **apprentice** at his brother's print shop, he would "borrow" books being printed there. The other apprentices would let him sneak books as long as he returned them in good condition the next morning. Ben confessed: "Often I sat up in my room reading the greatest part of the night . . ."

The kinds of books Ben read varied. As a very young boy, the Bible would have been his main reading material. But as he grew, other books interested him. They opened Ben to new ideas and skills. For example, Ben learned to swim, in part, by reading a book called *The Art of Swimming and Advice on Bathing,* by Melchi-sedec Thevenot. (It should be noted Ben did not actually read this book because it was written in French and, at the time, he didn't know French. Instead, he studied the illustrations in it to

> **After Ben decided to become a vegetarian, he convinced his brother, who he was living with, to give him the money that was saved from not buying extra meat.**

learn how to swim.) At age 16, after reading a book about vegetable diets, Ben was inspired to become a **vegetarian**. Ben's favorite book was *Pilgrim's Progress* by John Bunyan. This was a book about a man named Christian who travels to the Celestial City. It was the first fictional book Ben read, and he enjoyed the adventurous plot and dialogue.

Because Ben loved reading so much, it isn't surprising he invented some things that helped make the experience of reading books easier and more

Josiah Franklin

Josiah Franklin pulled his son out of formal schooling after only two years. Ben wrote he thought it was because college would cost too much money. Historians suspect, though, that his father simply realized Ben would never make a good minister, as he could be a bit mischievous. For example, as a child Ben found the long blessing before meals boring. One day, Ben suggested his dad simply bless the whole cask (or barrel) of food all at once. This, Ben reasoned, would save a lot of time!

As a young boy in Boston, Ben belonged to the Puritan Congregation. Puritans followed strict rules, such as wearing a certain color of clothes and not playing cards or drinking alcohol. They also believed in lots of Bible study and prayers; Ben and his family prayed for an hour every morning and evening and attended church services twice a week.

Words to Know

hornbook: a paddle-shaped piece of wood that colonial children used to learn to read and write.

apprentice: someone who agrees to work without pay for a certain amount of time for an artist or professional in return for learning a trade.

vegetarian: someone who doesn't eat meat.

bifocals: glasses with lenses that are divided into two parts. The upper half is for looking at things far away and the lower half magnifies things close up.

long arm: a mechanical arm that was used to reach books on high shelves.

enjoyable. One of his most famous inventions is **bifocals**. Ben invented bifocals later in life to solve a problem he was having.

As he got older, Ben needed two pairs of glasses. One pair was for seeing things that were close up, and one was for seeing things far away. He hated having to switch back and forth, calling the chore "troublesome." In 1784, he enlisted the help of a glasscutter and had the two pairs of lenses cut in half. Next, he glued the "distance" and "reading" lens together and called the invention Double Spectacles. Now, all Ben had to do was to look through the top lens to see things far away or the bottom lens when he wanted to read. He wrote about them in a letter to a friend, saying that he was "happy in the invention . . . which, serving for distant objects as well as near ones, make my eyes as useful to me as ever they were."

The name Junto came from junta, the Spanish word meaning "meeting."

Judging by the fact that bifocals are still used today, lots of other people have been happy with the invention, too!

Another useful invention Ben created was the **long arm**. Ben was especially proud of this invention, which he used to reach books on high shelves. The long arm was a pole with a gripper on the end. To open the gripper, the user pulled a piece of string or rope. Like bifocals, other people found this invention convenient, too. Today, we still use Ben's long arm, although the design has changed a bit. (Today, many "long arm" tools have a pincher device on the end that isn't operated with a cord. But the idea is the same.) Other useful reading inventions of Ben's include: a reading chair with a fan that was operated by a foot, a chair with a built-in step stool, and a chair with a small desk attached to one arm.

Words to Know

Junto: the social and civic club Ben Franklin formed with his friends and other businessmen.

shilling: currency, or money, used by early Americans.

As a successful printer in his twenties, Ben wanted to discuss books, politics, business, and other important city issues, so he formed a club called the **Junto**. Because it was made up mainly of tradesman, this group was also known as the Leather Apron Club. In addition to supporting each other, members of the Junto helped launch many positive changes and programs in Philadelphia. One of the programs Ben and the Junto helped create was the public library.

Ben's idea was for the members to pool their money to buy books they could all use. Each member paid an initial fee of 40 **shillings** to start the

fund and annual dues of 10 shillings to keep it going. In this way they created a library greater than any of them could individually afford. (Forty shillings was a good deal of money. For example, just 1 shilling would have bought about two meals in colonial times.) The money collected helped buy new books and pay for storing and maintaining them. During Ben's time, the Library Company of Philadelphia was open twice a week: on Saturdays from noon to 4 p.m. and on Wednesdays from 2 to 3 p.m. (Non-members could read the books but not take them home.) The library, which is still in existence, started off with 45 non-fiction books and now houses 500,000 books of all kinds of subjects and styles!

Make your own library "check out" system to help keep track of books when you lend them to friends. One simple system is to cut a business size envelope in half. Glue or tape one of the halves on the inside, back cover of your book. Next, add a small index card. When you lend a book to a friend, write down the book's title and your friend's name on the card and keep it somewhere safe until the book is returned. When you get the book back return the card to the pocket.

Colonial Americans used British currency. Research how many pence were in a shilling and how many shillings were in a pound in the 1700s.

Hold a drive to collect old prescription glasses for the Lions Club International, an organization that collects and distributes glasses to people who can't afford them.

Make Your Own
Spectacle Receptacle

Real bifocals would be tough to make since you'd need to cut glass. You can fashion your own "Ben Franklin glasses" using wire or pipe cleaners though. The lenses of Ben's famous glasses were small and round. You can keep track of your wire-rimmed glasses or sunglasses in this easy-to-make case.

✳CAUTION: Be very careful when using the glue gun and only use it with an adult's permission and help.

1 Turn on the hot glue gun so it has time to heat up. Cut the foam into a rectangle that is 7 by 9 inches.

2 Use the ruler to make small marks along one 9-inch side. Make marks at 3 inches and at 6 inches.

3 Fold the bottom third of the foam (at the 3-inch mark) so it lines up along the 6-inch mark. Use the hot glue gun to glue the short sides together. Do not glue the long side! When you're done, your case should look like an open envelope.

4 Put your glasses inside this envelope, then fold the top half of the foam over the pocket. The top edge of the case will not line up with the bottom edge.

This is okay; you need some space for your glasses. Make a tiny mark on the pocket so you know how far down the lid will come. Afterwards, take your glasses out of the case.

Supplies

✳ hot glue gun*

✳ 1 piece of 8½-by-11-inch craft foam, any color

✳ scissors

✳ ruler

✳ self-sticking Velcro

✳ sunglasses or other glasses

✳ sequins and glue, markers, or fabric paint

5 About ¼ to ½ inch from your mark, peel and stick one side of the Velcro to the case. (You can also hot glue the Velcro on to make it more secure.) Place the other piece of Velcro on the flap, so that when you close the flap the Velcro patches match up and stick together.

6 Use markers or fabric paint or glue sequins on your case to jazz it up! When you're done, you can protect your glasses in style.

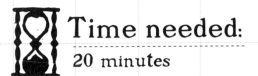

Time needed:
20 minutes

Make Your Own
Hornbook

Hornbooks were the paddle-shaped pieces of wood that colonial students used to learn the alphabet and reading. Some were very fancy, made out of silver or carved out of ivory. Most were simple, though, and had a hole in their handles so a string could be laced through and the books could be worn around the neck.

1 Lay the cardboard so that the 6-inch sides are on "top" and "bottom." At the top of the cardboard, make a mark at 2½ inches and a mark at 3½ inches.

2 From each mark, measure straight down 2 inches. From the end of each of these lines, draw a straight edge to the sides. Cut along all the lines to make your hornbook handle.

3 Cut the piece of paper to 5 by 5 inches. Next, write the alphabet (upper and lower case letters) and a favorite nursery rhyme, poem, or Bible verse. When you're finished, glue the paper in the middle of the paddle.

Tip: you only need just enough glue to keep the paper from moving around. You will secure it in the next step.

4 Trim your Contact paper to 5¼ by 5¼ inches. Peel off the back and carefully lay the contact paper, sticky side down, over the piece of paper with the alphabet. Smooth out any air bubbles with your fingers.

5 Poke a hole in the handle and add a piece of string. Now, you're ready to wear your hornbook and use it in class!

Supplies

* a piece of very thick cardboard, about 6 by 8 inches (You can also use a piece of balsa wood or foam board. If you use these materials, you'll also need a utility knife to cut them, but you must only use the utility knife with your parent's permission.)

* ruler

* scissors

* piece of white paper

* black marker

* glue or rubber cement

* Clear Contact™ Paper, about 6-by-6 inches

* string or yarn

Time needed:
20 minutes

Make Your Own
Long Arm

This project uses Super Glue and a drill, so you will need an adult's permission and help.

1 At one end of one of the 9-inch pieces of wood drill a hole. The hole should be in the middle and about 1 inch from the edge.

2 Use the Super Glue to attach the hinge to the two 9-inch pieces of wood. The hinge should be at the opposite end of the hole. When you're done, you should be able to open the 2 pieces of wood to make a "V."(You can attach the hinge with wood screws if you'd like. Just be careful to get screws that aren't long enough to go through your boards.) This piece will be your gripper. The end with the hinge is the bottom.

Supplies

* 2 pieces of flat wood around 9 inches long, 2½ inches wide, and ¼ inch thick

* drill

* 2-inch strap hinge from any hardware store

* Super Glue

* a piece of wood for the handle about ½ inch thick and 1½ inches wide, no longer than 3 feet long

* craft or wood glue

* Contact Grip Liner OR another gripping material

* scissors

* a cord as long as your handle like a leather shoe lace or a piece of rope

* 1 or 2 thick rubber bands, medium-sized

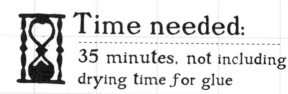

3 Attach the gripper to the handle with wood or craft glue. (You can use the Super Glue for this, too. It will dry more quickly.) The handle should go up about 3 inches from the bottom of the gripper and be on the side without the hole. Open the gripper.

4 Cut 2 pieces of Grip Liner and glue them to the entire inside of the gripper. This will make it easier to grab and hold on to things. Be sure to use craft glue because the grip material may have holes. If you use Super Glue and smooth the material down, your fingers will stick! Let the glue dry before moving on.

5 Keep the gripper open. Thread one end of your cord through the hole and make a knot. Note: you'll probably have to use a pair or scissors or a pen to gently poke a hole through the grip material.

6 Close the gripper and slide your rubber bands around the outsides. The rubber band will stop when it gets to the handle. (The more rubber bands you use, the stronger your long arm will be. Don't add too many rubber bands, though, or it will be too hard to open.)

7 To use your long arm, pull the cord to open the gripper to the desired width, then reach up and let the cord go to close the gripper around whatever object you want. The tension of the rubber band will close the gripper when you let go of the cord. Now, go grab something off a shelf!

Time needed:

35 minutes, not including drying time for glue

Printing Press

Once Ben and his father knew that the ministry was not for Ben, he no longer enrolled in school. Ben's father felt that he had to find something else for him to do. At first, Josiah had Ben come work in his candle and soap shop. Ben hated it.

After a couple of years Josiah decided Ben should apprentice at his older brother James' print shop. An apprentice is someone who agrees to work for a certain amount of time, without pay, in return for being taught a trade, craft, or business. The agreement was written and signed. At age 12, Ben went to work for James until he was 21 years old.

James and Ben didn't get along well. James was often cruel to Ben, even hitting him on occasion. But Ben did his best to learn the printing

Ben did not enjoy working for his older brother James. They did not get along.

business. James published a newspaper called the **New-England Courant**. In it, James often criticized things about society he didn't like, especially the governor of the colony. Sometimes, James used funny, fake names to

When Ben was little, he wanted to be a sailor like his oldest brother, Josiah Jr.

write articles or letters to the editor like Harry Meanwell, Fanny Mournful, or Tabitha Talkative, to name a few. At the time, it was against the law to speak out against the authorities, and so James was sent to jail more than once.

On one occasion when Ben was about halfway through his apprenticeship, James spoke out against some religious leaders and was arrested and thrown into jail for weeks. The colony's authorities wanted to take control of the paper away from James. To get around this problem, James publicly turned the newspaper over to Ben and released Ben from the apprenticeship. In reality, though, James was still in charge and Ben was still an apprentice.

Despite his young age (just 16), Ben did a good job of running the newspaper while his brother was in jail. He might have made a good partner for James, but that was not to be. When James was freed and returned to the paper, things were as tense as ever between them. One day, James and Ben got into a fight and Ben decided to quit. Even though he had the secret agreement to still be an apprentice,

Ben knew James couldn't make him honor it. To do so would mean everyone would know turning over the paper to Ben had been a lie. In anger, James told Ben he'd tell all the printers in Boston not to give him a job. So Ben ran away to New York in search of work.

When Ben got to New York he could not find a job there either. Someone suggested he try Philadelphia, and he took this suggestion. Ben fell in love with Philadelphia right away. It was bigger and livelier than Boston, and not long after arriving there he would consider it his hometown. In Philadelphia, Ben found work at a print shop run by a man named Samuel Keimer. Keimer, as Ben described in his autobiography, knew nothing of presswork. But Ben did and news of Ben's skill soon spread. One day a visitor came to the shop. It was the governor of Pennsylvania, Sir William Keith.

Silence Dogood

"Who is **Silence Dogood**?" This is exactly what Ben's brother James wanted to know when he started receiving letters to his newspaper from "her." Silence Dogood claimed to be a rural, middle-aged widow. Her letters were clever and funny and addressed things like religion, education, and women's rights. Silence's true identity was a topic James and his friends loved to debate. For six months, James found letters from this mysterious person shoved under the door of his print and newspaper shop. And then one day, Ben (who was just 16 at the time) admitted *he* was Silence Dogood all along! James, who already didn't get along very well with Ben, was very upset that his younger brother had fooled him and his friends.

While working in London, Ben got the nickname "Water-American." Ben's co-workers at the Palmer print shop called him this because he drank water instead of beer like they did.

Keith was impressed with Ben and suggested he set up his own print shop. Keith told Ben he should ask his father for the money he needed. Ben went home and asked but Josiah told Ben he should wait a few years. Either he didn't have the money to give Ben, or he didn't feel that Ben was ready to run a business of his own. Afterwards, Keith offered to help Ben set up the shop. He told Ben, "Give me an inventory of the things necessary to be had from England, and I will send for them." At the time, no one sold printing equipment in America. After Ben put together the list, Keith felt that Ben should check out the equipment before he purchased it. Keith promised to send letters of credit to Ben once he reached London. These letters of credit would allow Ben to purchase materials that Keith would pay for. But Keith never sent the letters. Ben ended up disappointed, far from home, and broke.

Ben and Deborah in Philadelphia after he returned from London.

The font (or style of lettering) known as Franklin Gothic was named after Ben Franklin.

Making the best of a tough situation, Ben found work with a famous London printer, Samuel Palmer. Later on, he took a job with another well-known London printer named John Watt. Ben spent almost two years in London. He made many friends, including a few lady friends, and seemed to forget all about Deborah Read who was back in America. Ben only wrote her once while he was gone, even though they'd talked about getting married. Deborah ended up getting married to someone else. In his autobiography Ben wrote that his time in London "transformed me from a boy who knew a bit about printing, into a master printer."

Busy-Body

Remember the Silence Dogood letters that got Ben so much attention? After Ben returned to Philadelphia and established himself in the printing business, he wanted to start his own newspaper. But there were already two newspapers in the city. One was published by Ben's former boss Samuel Keimer. Ben decided to try to get Keimer to leave the newspaper business. He did this by writing funny essays called the Busy-Body letters and publishing them in a competitor's newspaper! The letters were so popular that Keimer didn't just leave the newspaper business. He sold his paper, *The Universal Instructor in All Arts and Sciences and Pennsylvania Gazette*, to Ben for a bargain price! Ben renamed the paper *The Pennsylvania Gazette* and then turned it into the top newspaper in Philadelphia.

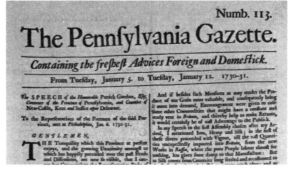

Words to Know

Ben returned to America in 1726 with the help of a man named Thomas Denham. Denham and Ben had become friends on the voyage to London. Upon their return to America together, they opened a general store, and Ben hoped to become wealthy. But then Thomas died suddenly and Ben was left with no money once again. Thomas had been the one to pay for the store and he did not leave it to Ben in his will. So Ben went back to work for Samuel Keimer's print shop, but again, it did not go well. Ben and Keimer didn't get along. Keimer wasn't a very good businessman, and this frustrated Ben. Eventually Ben quit and opened his own print shop with a couple of friends. When the friends left the business, Ben was on his own. He was only in his early twenties.

With his skill and passion, Ben became a highly successful and respected printer. His witty and popular newspaper, **The Pennsylvania Gazette**, was a great success. This is also the time period in which he began the club called Junto. By the early 1730s, Ben was the owner of three print shops. He and Deborah renewed their courtship (by this time, Deborah's first husband had disappeared). They started a family. While Ben worked in the print shop and wrote the newspaper, Deborah sold stationary, pens, and other items, such as the soap made by Ben's father in Boston, in the space next door.

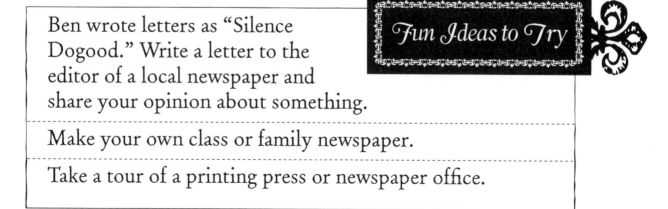

Fun Ideas to Try

Ben wrote letters as "Silence Dogood." Write a letter to the editor of a local newspaper and share your opinion about something.

Make your own class or family newspaper.

Take a tour of a printing press or newspaper office.

Make Your Own
Paper Mold and Paper

Today, paper is made out of wood. In Ben's day, paper was made with bits of fabric or rags. You can make your own paper using a combination of these things. Printers used a simple, two-piece device called a mold and deckle to form paper into uniform sizes. It looked kind of like a box within a box.

1 Stretch the window screen over the back of the frame. Staple the screen to the frame with the help of an adult. Pull the screen as tightly as you can.

2 Tear up the paper into small pieces, about 1-inch square. It doesn't matter if they are exactly square or exactly 1-inch. Tear up the other materials you've selected as well. Soak the pieces in warm water for about 30 minutes.

Supplies

* 8-by-10-inch wooden picture frame
* 10-by-12-inch piece of window screen
* staple gun*
* scrap paper and bits of material like toilet or tissue paper, napkins, construction paper, white lined or unlined writing paper, old greeting cards, newspaper, bits of foil, ribbon or scrap fabric
* plastic tub or basin
* blender OR food processor
* liquid starch
* sponge
* kitchen towel OR piece of felt

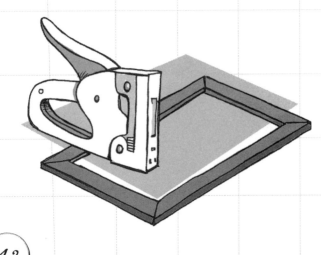

Caution: Use only with the permission and supervision of an adult.

3 Fill your blender or food processor about three-quarters to the top with clean water.

4 Place a handful of wet paper and materials and add to the blender. Mix on high for approximately 30 seconds. Keep adding the paper mixture and blending in 30-second intervals until you have the desired amount of pulp. The pulp should look like lumpy oatmeal when you're done.

5 Fill the basin halfway with fresh water. Add a few teaspoons of starch to the water and mix it together. This step is called "sizing." The starch will keep ink from bleeding, or spreading, on the paper. Next, pour the pulp into the water and swish it around a bit so it's not clumped together.

6 Carefully dip your mold into the basin and under the pulp. Collect the pulp on top of the screen and use your hand to gently spread it around the mold evenly.

7 Lift the mold out of the basin and let the water drain off. You can use the sponge to push any extra water out.

8 After you have gotten all the water you can out of the paper, lay the kitchen towel over the mold. Keep one hand on the towel and use the other hand to flip the mold over. The paper should fall out of the mold onto the towel. If it doesn't, gently pull the edges.

9 Lay the piece of paper flat on the towel or on some newspaper. If it's sunny, you can put the paper outside to dry more quickly. Use any remaining pulp to make more pieces of paper. You can keep extra pulp in a sealed container for a couple of days. When you're ready to use it again, just add a little water. When the paper is completely dry, it's ready to write on! Do not put any pulp down the drain as it will clog your pipes.

 Time needed:

35 minutes, not including soaking and drying time

Make Your Own Letterpress

Printing was a physically demanding and time-consuming process for printers. Newspapers and pages had to be pressed one at a time. To make a page, a printer first lined up all the letters in a tray called a composing stick. Next, he spread ink over the tray and put paper on top. Then, he lowered the press so the ink would stick to the paper. Afterwards, the printer hung the page up to dry. Here's an easy way to make your own letterpress.

1 Spread the newspaper over your work area. Cut the potato in half lengthwise. If it's large enough, you might be able to cut it into thirds to make more letterpresses.

2 Use the pen to outline a letter or shape on each end of the potatoes. Your shape or letter will print backwards, so draw it backwards to begin with.

3 Carefully cut away the potato so that the shape or letter you want is raised about ¼ to ½ inch high.

4 Dab the sponge in the paint and then dab the sponge onto the letter or shape.

5 Press the potato carefully on the paper. Don't press too hard, though, or you might break the potato.

6 Have fun and experiment with your letterpresses! See if you can print your name or create your very own homemade stationery.

Supplies

* newspaper
* sweet potatoes or large baking potatoes (sweet potatoes work a little better because they are firmer)
* utility knife*
* pen or pencil
* acrylic paint, any color
* sponge
* homemade paper

Time needed:

45 minutes, not including drying time

*Caution: Use only with the permission and supervision of an adult.

Paper Money

While the British ruled the American colonies, the colonists used silver and gold coins for money. England made a lot of rules about what could and could not happen in the colonies. That's why a lot of people living there wanted independence from England.

Since the British wouldn't allow the colonists to make their own coins and didn't ship many coins over to America, there was a shortage of money. This was a real problem for the colonists who were trying to build a country because there wasn't an easy way to pay for goods or services. Sometimes they used tobacco leaves to pay for things or they used a **bartering** system.

Ben Franklin believed paper **currency** was the answer. He had noticed the advantages of paper money while living in

London. He argued that it was easier to carry around and easier to use—and that for these reasons people would be more likely to spend it. Spending would help improve the economy and, in turn, everyone's lives. Ben further argued that the only people who didn't want paper currency were the wealthy. In a famous pamphlet called "A Modest Enquiry into the Nature and Necessity of a Paper Currency" Ben wrote down all his thoughts on paper currency. One thing Ben didn't mention, of course, was that the job of printing money would

Words to Know

bartering: a system where people exchange goods or services for other goods or services.

currency: another name for money.

counterfeiters: people who copy money or make fake money and use it as real money.

engraving: a type of printing where the design is etched or drawn *into* the plate instead of having the letters or design raised on the plate.

frugal: a way to describe someone who is careful not to overspend money or waste resources.

Ben printed pictures of leaves on the back of the money he designed for Pennsylvania. On the front of the bills was the coat of arms for the Penn family, the family who owned and ran Pennsylvania at the time.

probably make *him* wealthy! In any case, people started to warm up to the idea of paper money, and in 1730 the Pennsylvania Assembly asked Ben to print it. Eventually other colonies, such as New Jersey, asked Ben to print money for them, too.

In Ben's time, just like today, the biggest challenge with creating paper money was making sure that **counterfeiters** would not be able to copy it. Ben's idea for making money difficult to

Famous Sayings

Here are some famous (and not so famous) quotes from Ben Franklin about money:

"A penny saved is a penny earned."

"The use of money is all the advantage there is in having money."

"Keep thy shop, and thy shop will keep thee."

"If you'd know the value of money, go and borrow some."

"Great spenders are bad lenders."

"Rather go to bed supperless than run in debt for a breakfast."

"He who multiplies riches multiplies cares."

"Beware of little expenses: a small leak will sink a great ship."

Ben Franklin appears on the front of the U.S. $100 bill.
The $100 bill is currently the highest denomination
in public circulation, but the highest
denomination ever printed by the United States was the
$100,000 bill. It featured a portrait of President
Wilson and was used only between banks.

copy was to make the designs very intricate. Using a technique he'd seen in London, Ben engraved a copper printing plate with highly detailed leaf patterns. Printers used copper because it's a soft metal and easy to **engrave**. Along with creating elaborate leaf designs, some experts believe Ben tried to foil counterfeiters by spelling the word "Pennsylvania" in different ways.

Money Today

Since 1877, the U.S. Department of the Treasury's Bureau of Engraving and Printing has printed all the U.S. currency. What once started out as a small, six-person operation, now has over 2,000 employees. Money and postal stamps are printed 24 hours a day! (Most of the bills are used to replace worn out currency.) Like in colonial times, counterfeit bills are still a challenge. Over the years, the Department of the Treasury has tried to prevent people from printing fake money in a variety of ways. Some of these ways include: using a hard-to-copy green ink, weaving tiny threads into the paper, using watermarks, engraving tiny words or pictures within the design (microprinting), and printing serial numbers and treasury seals on the bills.

Three women have appeared on U.S. currency at some point in history. See if you can find out who they are. (Hints: one appeared on early paper money and two appear on recent coins.)

Use a magnifying glass to examine bills and coins. Can you see Abe Lincoln inside the Lincoln Memorial on the back of a penny?

Pretend the United States is going to create a new denomination of money. Write a letter explaining why you feel your favorite historical person should be featured on the bill or coin. (There is a law that says no living person's likeness can be on U.S. money.)

It's hard to believe that a master printer and genius like Ben Franklin would misspell the name of his own state, if it weren't intentional.

The contracts to print paper currency made Ben a good deal of money. Even after he became wealthy, Ben had strong beliefs about money. He believed in spending money wisely and being practical. He also believed "the pursuit of money for no purpose" was improper. He was proud of his **frugal** ways and proud he had chosen a frugal wife as well. For a long time, the Franklins had no servants, and Ben wore clothes Deborah made herself. Despite Ben and Deborah's desire for practical spending, they both enjoyed the finer things in life and sometimes got caught up in appearances. For example, one day Deborah served Ben his oatmeal in a china bowl instead of his regular, plain bowl. When Ben asked her about it, she admitted to spending a good deal of money on it (23 shillings) just because she felt Ben deserved to eat in a fancy bowl like their neighbors. It bothered Ben, but in the years to come, he and Deborah would own a complete set of expensive china and other things that, at a younger age, Ben would have considered a waste of money.

Make Your Own
Watermarked Bill

A watermark is a special design on a piece of paper (such as a dollar bill or a piece of stationary) that is embedded into the paper itself. They are a part of the security measures taken by the Treasury Department to discourage counterfeiters. For example, on the $100 bill, there is a watermark of a smaller Ben Franklin next to the Ben Franklin portrait. You can see watermarks when you hold the piece of paper up to light. Of course, you can't make money to use in stores or banks. But you can make your own paper money to use at home or with your friends for fun.

1 Using the black pen, draw the design you'd like to be your watermark on the piece of paper. Your watermark can be anything you'd like, such as your lucky number, your initial, or a shape. Just be careful not to make it bigger than your 5-by-7-inch frame and be careful not to make it too detailed. A heavily detailed design will be difficult to trace with glue.

Supplies

* piece of white paper
* black pen
* a piece of 7-by-9-inch piece of window screen
* waterproof wood glue OR puff paint found with the fabric paint in most craft stores
* wax paper
* a 5-by-7-inch wooden frame
* a staple gun*
* the directions for homemade paper found in the previous chapter
* green food coloring (optional)
* markers for decorating

Caution: Use only with an adult's help and permission.

2 Once you've drawn a watermark, lay the screen over the piece of paper. Next, use the waterproof glue to "trace" over the design. After tracing the design, carefully pick the screen off the white paper and put it on a piece of wax paper to dry. Allow the glue to dry completely.

3 When the glue is dry, attach the screen to the back of the wooden frame using the staple gun. Make sure you pull the screen tight and be sure your watermark design is facing inside the frame. You now have a paper money mold!

4 Follow the directions in the previous chapter to make paper pulp. You can add a few drops of green food coloring to the pulp while it's still in the blender if you'd like your money to be green.

5 Use your new money mold to scoop up some pulp. Because of the watermark, you will want to make sure you push out all the extra water you can with the sponge. If you don't, the water may cause the paper to fill in the watermark.

6 Carefully turn the mold over and let your money dry completely. When it's ready, you can decorate the bill. Maybe you can draw your own portrait on it or special microprinting around the edges. Have some fun designing it!

Time needed:

30 minutes, not including drying time

Make Your Own

Invisible Ink

The U.S. Bureau of Engraving and Printing uses special ink when printing money. This ink is difficult to copy. Here is an easy, "invisible" ink you can make yourself to keep other people from reading or copying what you've written.

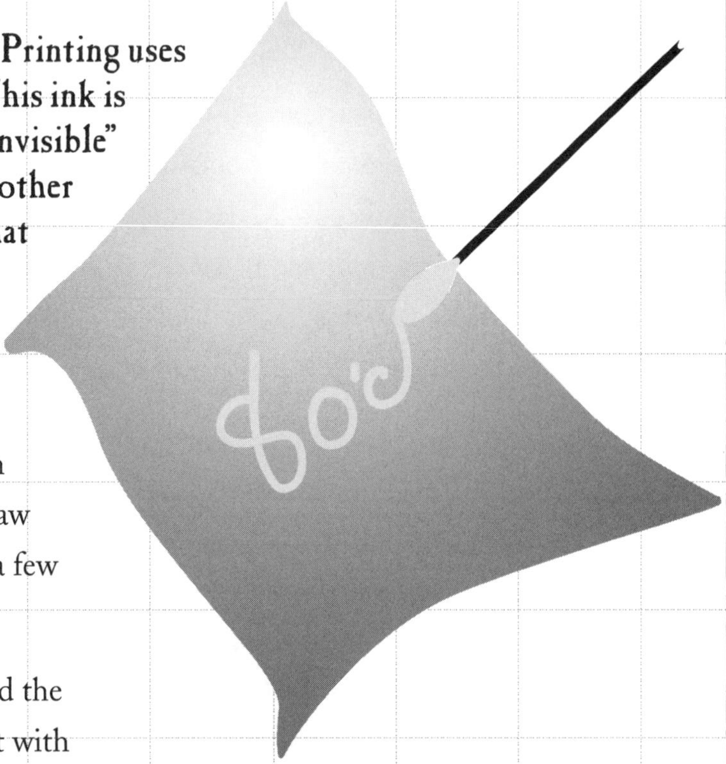

1 First, lightly chew the end of the toothpick to make a small "brush." Dip the toothpick or Q-tip in the lemon juice and write a note or draw a picture. Let the lemon juice dry for a few minutes.

2 To see the "invisible" message, hold the paper up to a light bulb or warm it with another heat source, such as a blow dryer. Be careful not to burn your hands!

3 The message should now be visible. This works because the lemon juice has acid in it, and the acid weakens the paper. When the paper is placed near a heat source, the weakened parts turn brown faster than the rest of the paper.

Supplies

* toothpick OR Q-tip
* lemon juice
* piece of paper

Time needed:
5 minutes

Poor Richard's Almanac

Almanacs are reference books containing information such as weather forecasts, lists and tables, moon phases and tide charts, and short articles and tips. In colonial times, **almanacs** were nearly as popular as the Bible. These were the only books that many families owned.

Because almanacs were very popular and because they were published every year, almanacs were big business for colonial printers. The majority of printers published their own almanacs. Ben Franklin, who was a smart business-man, was no exception. While his desire to make money from an almanac wasn't different from any other printer's, the almanac that he created *was* different.

Along with the usual forecasts and household tips, Ben's almanac had jokes, riddles, funny essays, and sayings. Remember when Ben's brother used fake names to publish articles and letters? Ben did the

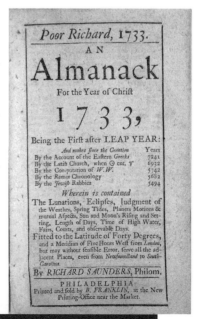

Poor Richard, 1733: An Almanack
For the Year of Christ 1973.

Two pages from Poor Richard's Almanack for 1736.

same thing. The author of Ben's almanac was a made-up character named **Richard Saunders**. Because of this, the book was known as *Poor Richard's Almanac*. Like Ben, Richard was clever and had a sly sense of humor. For example, he "predicted" when one of Ben's **rivals** would die. Ben could write things like this because he was writing under a pen name. All he had to do was blame Richard Saunders. Of course, many people, including the rival, knew the truth! Ben sometimes wrote as Poor Richard's wife, Bridget. She offered advice, too. Sometimes she and Richard would argue. Once, Bridget complained about their fights being so public. She wrote: "Cannot I have a little fault or two but all the country must see it in print?" The colonists found this bickering a lot of fun to read.

Ben borrowed the name Poor Richard's Almanac from his brother James' almanac called Poor Robin's Almanac.

Poor Richard's Almanac was also widely known for its **maxims**. Maxims are sayings or little bits of wisdom to live by. Ben didn't really write all of the sayings in his almanac. Most of them were proverbs from the Bible or from other sources. In his autobiography, Ben said the sayings came from "many ages and nations." But Ben often changed them and made them funnier or easier to understand. For example, he changed the saying "Fresh fish and new-come guests smell, but that they are three days old." Ben's version was "Fish and visitors stink in three days."

Poor Richard's Maxims

❋ Haste makes waste

❋ No gains without pains

❋ A penny saved is a penny earned

❋ God helps them that help themselves

❋ He that lies down with dogs shall rise up with fleas

❋ Early to bed and early to rise makes a man healthy, wealthy, and wise

❋ A good example is the best sermon

❋ The use of money is all the advantage there is in having money

❋ The sleeping fox catches no poultry

❋ Eat to live, live not to eat

❋ He does not possess wealth, it possesses him

❋ Half the truth is often a great lie

❋ Necessity never made a good bargain

❋ If you'd know the value of money, go and borrow some

❋ He that would catch fish, must venture his bait

❋ He who multiplies riches multiplies cares

❋ Forewarned is forearmed

❋ Don't throw stones at your neighbor's if your own windows are glass

❋ Well done is better than well said

Many of Poor Richard's maxims were about money. This wasn't an accident. Throughout his life, Ben had a desire to help people lead more frugal and practical lives. He believed pursuing money just for the sake of having money wasn't good for individuals or society. In his final edition of *Poor Richard's Almanac*, Ben gathered together all the sayings about money he had published over the years. Next, he put them into a story about a made-up character named Father Abraham who made a speech during an auction. The story poked fun about how hard it was to convince men and women to be frugal (or to save and spend money wisely). The colonists enjoyed the story so much that, later on, Ben published it by itself. This time, the story was called

Ben's almanac cost two shillings per dozen.

Father Abraham's Speech. The story was also published under the title of *The Way to Wealth.* The story was popular around the world and published in other languages including French and German. Because of its success, Ben Franklin's name became linked with frugality and hard work.

Despite having a reputation for frugality, even Ben admitted he first wrote his almanac to make money. In his first edition, he playfully wrote: "I might in this place attempt to gain thy favor by declaring that I write almanacs with no other view than that of the public good, but in this I should not be sincere. The plain truth of the matter is, I am excessively poor and my wife . . . has threatened more than once to burn all my books . . . if I do not make some profitable use of them for the good of my family."

Virtues to Live By

Ben wanted to help others improve their lives, but he wanted to improve himself as well. As part of a plan to reach what he called "moral perfection," Ben came up with a list of 13 **virtues** (or good personality traits) he wanted to live his life by. To keep track of how well he was doing, Ben carried a notebook and, later on, ivory tablets. If he didn't do well in a particular area, he made a mark in the column for that day. It was hard to achieve all the virtues at once, and Ben discovered he couldn't be perfect! In his autobiography he wrote: "I soon found I had undertaken a task more difficult than I had imagined. While my care was employed in guarding against one fault, I was often surprised by another . . ."

Here are some of the virtues Ben aspired to:

Temperance: Eat not to dullness; drink not to elevation.

Silence: Speak not but what may benefit others or yourself; avoid trifling conversations.

Order: Let all your things have their places; each part of your business its time.

But later on, once he saw how popular his almanac was, Ben decided to use it to make a positive difference in the lives of people. In his autobiography he wrote: "I endeavored to make it both entertaining and useful . . . and observing that it was generally read . . . I considered it as a proper vehicle for conveying instruction among the common people . . ."

Ben wrote and published *Poor Richard's Almanac* from 1732 until 1758. According to Ben's autobiography, it sold nearly 10,000 copies a year! Along with *The Way to Wealth*, *Poor Richard's Almanac* made Ben a very wealthy man. Ben was so wealthy, in fact, that he was able to retire from printing in his early forties.

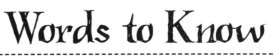

Words to Know

almanac: reference book containing weather forecasts, lists and tables, moon phases and tide charts, short articles, and household tips.
Richard Saunders: the pen name Ben used to author his almanac.
rival: somebody you compete against.
maxims: sayings or little bits of wisdom.
virtues: positive personality traits.

Resolution: Resolve to perform what you ought; perform without fail what you resolve.

Industry: Lose no time; be always employed in something useful.

Frugality: Make no expense but to do good; waste nothing.

Sincerity: Use no hurtful deceit; think innocently and justly.

Justice: Wrong none by doing injuries, or omitting the benefits that are your duty.

Moderation: Avoid extremes; forbear resenting injuries so much as think they deserve.

Tranquility: Be not disturbed at trifles, or at accidents, common or unavoidable.

Cleanliness: Tolerate no uncleanness in body, clothes, or habitation.

Make Your Own
Piggy Bank

Ben Franklin said, "A penny saved is a penny earned." With a piggy bank this will be a lot easier to do!

1 Cover your work area with newspaper and remove the milk jug lid. Your lid will be your piggy bank's snout, so don't throw it out.

2 If you are using empty paper rolls, cut them in half so there are four "feet." Turn the milk jug on its side and glue the paper rolls or empty spool feet on to the top. It should look like your "pig" is lying on its back with its feet in the air.

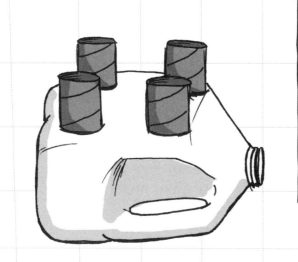

Supplies

❋ 1-gallon, plastic milk jug and cap, cleaned and dried

❋ 2 empty toilet paper rolls OR 4 empty thread spools

❋ Super Glue*

❋ newspaper

❋ papier-mâché (2 cups of all-purpose flour mixed with 2 cups of water in a bowl)

❋ waxed paper

❋ 1 pink pipe cleaner (or another color of your choosing)

❋ pink acrylic paint (or another color of your choosing)

❋ black permanent marker

❋ utility knife*

*Caution: Use only with an adult's help and permission.

3 Wad up a piece of newspaper and stuff it under and around the jug handle. You're going to cover it, so don't worry if it's not perfect. You just need enough paper to fill in that area so your pig is nice and round.

4 Tear a couple of sections of newspaper into strips about 1 inch wide and several inches long. Dip the strips into your papier-mâché and remove any extra mixture with your fingers. Now, begin laying the strips on the jug in a collage fashion all around the plastic. Do NOT cover the opening of the milk jug. You will need several layers of papier-mâché.

5 Reinforce the pig's feet with extra layers of papier-mâché, especially if you are using paper towel rolls. Your piggy bank will be heavy when it's full of coins.

6 Once you've put on several layers of paper, carefully turn the piggy bank over and place it on a piece of waxed paper. Your bank should now look like a pig standing on four legs. Add several papier-mâché layers to the top of the bank. You can make pig ears by covering triangular pieces of cardboard with papier-mâché and adding them to the top of the jug.

7 Allow the bank to completely dry. Depending on how many layers you made or how humid it is, this might take several days.

8 When everything is dry, paint your piggy bank and add a curly piece of pipe cleaner for a tail.

9 Replace the milk cap and use the marker to draw holes for the "snout" and a couple of eyes and a mouth. Now, you're ready to start saving! You can cut a money slot in the top of your piggy bank using a utility knife or just take off the cap to add or take out money.

Time needed:

60 minutes, not including drying time for papier-mâché and paint

Make Your Own "Frugal" Frame

Ben Franklin preached that people should be frugal, and he didn't like to see things go to waste. He would have loved the idea of recycling! Here's a project that puts old puzzles to good use and helps keep them out of landfills. While the frame you create is drying, you can illustrate your favorite Poor Richard maxim on the back of a paper grocery bag. Reusing paper bags is another great way to recycle. And when you're done, you can display your work in the frame.

1 Cover your work area with newspaper. If you put your puzzle together before you paint it, the painting will go more quickly and won't be as messy, but you can also paint the pieces separately. Feel free to add glitter or bits of foil or ribbon while the paint is still wet. That way the glitter and other stuff will stick better. Make sure to let the paint dry before you break the pieces apart.

2 While the jigsaw pieces are drying, carefully cut out the middle of the cardboard to make a frame that's about 2 inches wide on all sides.

Supplies

* newspaper
* an old jigsaw puzzle*
* craft paint in various colors
* glitter, bits of foil or ribbon (optional)
* a medium-sized piece of thick cardboard OR an old, wooden frame
* scissors
* glue
* an old shoelace or a piece of yarn

*It doesn't matter if the puzzle pieces are big or small, or if your puzzle is missing pieces. You can even combine several puzzles.

3 Glue the ends of shoelace or ribbon on the back of the frame. This is what you can use to hang the frame.

4 When the puzzle pieces are dry, take them apart and glue them onto the cardboard or wooden frame collage style. Overlap pieces or mix and match colors or sizes to create a cool effect. Now, you're ready to add your artwork to the frame! Use a photograph, an illustrated picture of one of Poor Richard's maxims, or anything your imagination can think of. Use leftover puzzle pieces to make more frames or decorate an old box.

Time needed:

35 minutes, not including drying time

Fun Ideas to Try

In his autobiography, Ben wrote about his almanac: "I endeavored to make it both entertaining and useful . . ." Invent something new that is both entertaining and useful.

Read an almanac or a copy of *Poor Richard's Almanac.*

Out of all the virtues Ben wished to have, he found "Order" and "Humility" the two hardest to achieve. Which of Ben's virtues do you find the most challenging? Make a chart to keep track of how well you can achieve one of Ben's virtues.

Ben's almanac was a bestseller. Find out which books are on the Bestseller List this week or were on the list the week you were born.

Start a recycling program at school or at home or in your neighborhood.

The Gulf Stream Map

When Ben was a young boy, he wanted to be a sailor. His older brother, Josiah Jr., had been one. Because Josiah died at sea, Ben's father steered Ben away from ship life. This didn't stop Ben from loving the ocean, though. And it was this love that helped Ben make a significant contribution to sea travel. What was this important contribution? A map of the **Gulf Stream**.

Ben Franklin's chart of the Gulf Stream.

The Gulf Stream is one the world's longest and strongest ocean **currents**. Within the stream, the water is warmer than the water on either side of it. It moves along the southern and eastern coasts of the United States, through the Atlantic Ocean and toward Newfoundland and England. The earth's rotation and the sun's heat and light make the Gulf Stream the way it is, and then the Gulf Stream affects the weather of the East Coast of the United States as well as the other coasts it travels near. The amount of water moving within the Gulf Stream is

The Spanish explorer Ponce de León was one of the first people to observe and write about the Gulf Stream. He did this in the early 1500s.

huge. It is much bigger than the Nile, the Amazon, the Mississippi, and all other major rivers combined!

Observing the Gulf Stream wasn't something Ben did in just one or two days. Rather, over the course of many years and voyages across the Atlantic,

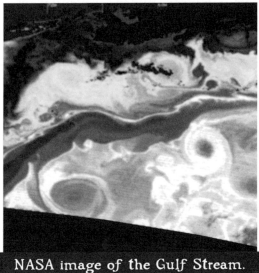

NASA image of the Gulf Stream.

Ben observed the Gulf Stream. For instance, he noted the water in the Gulf Stream current was a different color than the water around it, and that it had a lot of seaweed in it. He also noticed that the whales liked to swim near it. The current's warmer water temperatures caused these things. Later, when Ben was the **Postmaster General** of the United States he decided to study the current seriously.

Even though Ben had only basic scientific instruments, Ben's temperature and flow chart of the Gulf Stream were pretty accurate. Today, scientists use special satellites to see the Gulf Stream temperatures in the different color water from space.

The Gulf Stream is sometimes called the "river in the ocean." This is because, in many ways, the current acts like a river. For example, it has tributaries, which are small bodies of water that flow into a larger body of water. Just like a river.

Ben decided to study the Gulf Stream as the Postmaster General because the Gulf Stream was affecting mail service! Ben noticed that mail sent from America to England was delivered much quicker than mail sent from England to America. Sometimes this difference in delivery time was several weeks.

Ben didn't have a good explanation for this, so he asked his cousin, a whaling captain named Timothy Folger, if he had any ideas. Folger told Ben about the current. Many whalers like Folger knew about the current and used it to their advantage while hunting whales.

Ben was Postmaster General for all the American colonies from 1753 to 1774.

Ben traveled back and forth between America and England many times for business and political reasons. During his last couple of voyages, Ben began mapping out the Gulf Stream. He did so by lowering a thermometer over the ship's side and taking the water temperature. To find out the temperature of deeper depths, Ben lowered a barrel with a valve that opened when the water pressure reached

Words to Know

Gulf Stream: one of the world's longest and strongest ocean currents, affecting both sea travel and weather in several continents.

current: a body of water that is moving in a certain direction.

Postmaster General: an official in charge of a country's post office department or agency.

journal: a magazine or publication a group or organization publishes for its members.

Ben named the current the Gulf Stream because it begins in the Gulf of Mexico.

a certain level. Water pressure gets higher the deeper you go. After the water filled the barrel, Ben pulled it up and looked at the thermometer. Since the Gulf Stream had warmer temperatures, Ben could accurately map out where it was. When he wrote about his observations, Ben noted, "It will appear from them that the thermometer may be an useful instrument to a navigator . . ."

Using his own scientific observations and information from his cousin, Ben published the Franklin/Folger map of the Gulf Stream in 1786. It appeared as part of an article titled "Maritime Observations and a Chart of the Gulph Stream," in a **journal** called *The Transactions of the American Philosophical Society*. As part of the instructions for avoiding the Gulf Stream Ben wrote, "A stranger may know when he is in the Gulph Stream by the warmth of the water which is greater than that of the water on each side of it. If then he is bound to the westward, he should cross the stream to get out of it as soon as possible." Unfortunately, for unknown reasons, many of the mail ship captains didn't use the map and ignored Ben's advice about avoiding the Gulf Stream. As a result, the mail from England continued to arrive late.

Ben testing the temperature of the water on his way from America to England.

Make Your Own
Thermometer

Ben Franklin probably used a mercury thermometer to measure the Gulf Stream's temperature. Mercury is poisonous, but here is a way to make your own thermometer using rubbing alcohol. This thermometer works because the alcohol expands and contracts as it is heated and cooled. As the alcohol warms and expands it rises up the straw. As it cools, it sinks down the straw.

1 Put an equal amount of water and rubbing alcohol in the bottle until the mixture reaches about 2 inches high.

2 Add a few drops of food coloring. Carefully swirl the bottle to mix the water, alcohol, and food coloring together.

3 Put the straw into the bottle and water-alcohol-food coloring mixture. Arrange the straw so that it is not touching the bottom of the bottle.

4 Use the modeling clay to form a seal around the straw at the neck of the bottle and help the straw stay in position. The straw should be standing straight up.

5 Now you're ready to try out your thermometer. Just place it someplace warm and watch what happens!

Supplies

* water
* rubbing alcohol
* a short, clear bottle (plastic or glass) with a narrow neck
* red food coloring
* a clear straw
* a small bit of modeling clay

Time needed:
20 minutes

Make Your Own
Wave Bottle

Ben learned about the Gulf Stream by observing the ocean. Here's an easy way to create your own mini "ocean" to observe.

1 Add about 1 inch of sand to your bottle. You can add some tiny shells if you'd like, too.

2 Fill about half the bottle with water, then add a few drops of the food coloring, then about 2 or 3 inches of baby oil.

3 Screw on the lid and put a piece of duct tape around the lid to seal it tight. Now, your mini ocean is ready to watch! Just tilt it back and forth to watch the waves and sand move.

Supplies

* sand
* 20-ounce clear, plastic bottle with a screw-on lid
* water
* blue food coloring
* baby oil
* duct tape

Time needed:
10 minutes

Electricity and the Lightning Rod

fter Ben retired from the printing business in 1748, he had plenty of time and money to devote to what he called "philosophical studies and amusements." This included his study of **electricity**, a topic that absolutely fascinated him.

In Ben's day, electricity was a mysterious thing. No one understood how it might be used. Some scientists of the day believed there were two kinds of electricity, one that pulled things and one that pushed things. Today, we know the movement of **electrons** between **atoms** causes electricity and the number of electrons inside an atom makes it negatively or positively charged. And some folks used these push-pull properties of electricity to perform funny shows or demonstrations. For example, they might make an object "dance" or make static electricity fly off a person. Ben watched one such demonstration put on by a Scottish scientist named Archibald Spencer.

In his autobiography, Ben wrote he was so surprised and pleased by Dr. Spencer's show that he bought the scientist's equipment. Then, he set up his own home laboratory to do electrical experiments.

Many of Ben's experiments involved static electricity. Static electricity is electricity that is not moving in a **circuit**. In order to produce the sparks of electricity he needed, Ben made some-

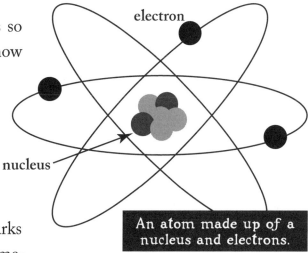

An atom made up of a nucleus and electrons.

thing he called an electrostatic machine. This machine had a revolving, glass globe that rubbed against a chamois skin, which is a kind of leather. Static electricity built up inside the globe. Knitting needles then pulled the charge out of the jar and into Leyden jars. These were special storage jars—made of glass, foil, wires, and water—that stored electricity. Using this machine, Ben had two friends draw off charges from the globe and then touch each other to see if they could pass the sparks back and forth. This experiment resulted in two very important discoveries. First, that electricity was a single thing and not two different forces. This is called the single-fluid theory of electricity. And second, that electricity generated equal positive and negative charges. In other words, there couldn't be a bigger positive charge than a negative charge or vice versa; they were always in balance. This is called the conservation of charge. These discoveries caused a huge buzz in the science world. Ben wrote about this experiment and others in letters. Years later, a friend gathered those letters into a book called *Experiments and Observations on Electricity*. This book was translated into French, German, and Italian, and it made Ben Franklin famous among scientists worldwide.

Ben coined many terms we still use today: "positive and negative charge," "electrical battery," "conductor," and "shock."

Words to Know

electricity: energy created by the movement of electrons between atoms.

electrons: particles that, along with protons and the nucleus, make an atom.

atoms: tiny particles of matter that make up everything.

circuit: a system of conductors forming a path for electricity to move.

lightning rod: a device that attracts lightning and carries it into the ground and away from a building, invented by Ben Franklin in 1753.

conductor: a material through which electricity moves.

Because Ben noticed similarities between how lightning and electricity looked, behaved, and smelled, he suspected they were the same thing. To test his theory, Ben performed one of his most famous electrical experiments. During an early summer thunderstorm in 1752, he tied a brass key to the end of a kite string and headed outside with his son William, who was around 20 years old at the time. Once outside, he let the kite out in an open field and waited. Don't ever do this yourself, as it is very dangerous! Ben and his son took a huge risk of getting hit by lightning. As the story goes, the pair was just about to go home when Ben noticed some loose threads of the string standing up. This meant that the kite had collected the electrical charges in the clouds. When Ben touched the brass key with his knuckles, he got quite a shock!

Always a practical and helpful man, Ben put this discovery to use by inventing the **lightning rod**. A lightning rod is metal pole that attracts lightning and leads it into the ground, away from

Ben used metal rods and hemp to make his kite because they are good conductors. A conductor is a material that allows electricity to flow or move well.

buildings. This was an especially useful thing in colonial times since most homes and buildings were made of wood! If they were struck by lightning they would often burn to the ground, and the fire would often spread to surrounding houses as well. Ben described his new invention and gave installation instructions in his *Poor Richard's Almanac*. He wrote, "One should fix at the highest parts [of a building or home], rods of iron made sharp as a needle . . . and from the foot of these needles, a wire down the outside of the building into the ground thus drawing the electricity away from the building and protecting them from lightning."

Today, people all over the world use lightning rods. But in Ben's day, many folks didn't trust them. Some worried that drawing lightning into the ground could cause earthquakes. This didn't bother Ben. He was confident in his invention and proudly put up a lightning rod on his own home. And, on at least one occasion, the invention saved Ben's own house from a lightning strike!

Fun and Danger

Ben had fun with electricity. He liked to entertain guests by using it to move pretend spiders and fish and to surprise people standing around his yard by wiring up his iron fence to spark. He also created bells that sounded a warning when a storm was approaching. Ben admitted these bells often annoyed his wife!

Of course, working or playing with electricity is dangerous, and on many occasions Ben learned this the hard way. An example of this came one day when Ben decided to kill a turkey for some friends by electrical shock. Ben described the result as "a universal blow throughout my whole body from head to foot" and a "violent quick shaking of my body." After recovering the next day, Ben joked that he nearly cooked an old goose instead of a turkey.

Make Your Own
Potato Battery

This battery works because the copper in the pennies and the zinc in the nails react to each other. The chemical energy is converted to electric energy as electrons move through the potatoes.

1 Insert half of a penny in one end of potato #1. Insert approximately ½ inch of the nail into the other end of the potato. Do the same with potato #2.

2 Use the scissors to carefully strip the plastic casing off the ends of the copper wire. You'll need about an inch or more of exposed wire at each end.

3 Wrap one end of the copper wire around the nail in potato #1, and wrap the other end of the copper wire around the penny in potato #2.

4 Next, gently pull the LED wires in opposite directions. Be careful not to pull them out of the bulb.

5 Hold the LED bulb gently with your fingers so that the nail touches one of the wires or posts, and the penny touches the other wire or post. (Don't worry about your fingers accidentally touching the wire. The battery doesn't have enough volts to shock you.)

6 The LED should light up! LED lights are not very bright. If you can't see it, cup your hands around the bulb. Note: Electricity moves through a LED

Supplies

✳ 2 small, baking potatoes, labeled #1 and #2

✳ 2 shiny pennies, cleaned with steel wool or buffed with a pencil eraser

✳ 2 galvanized nails, 2 inches long

✳ 1 piece of insulated copper wire, approximately 3 inches long

✳ scissors

✳ 1 or 2-volt LED light from an electronic store or hobby shop. It must have 2 posts or wires hanging from the bottom. (One wil be positive; the other will be negative)

light in only one direction. If the bulb doesn't light up, it might be because the positive and negative sides switched. Try touching the wires to the opposite sides. For instance if one LED wire was touching the nail, have it touch the penny instead.

Time needed:
10 minutes

Make Your Own Kite

1 Use the utility knife to carve notches into the very tops and bottoms of each wooden dowel. Then lay the shorter dowel 8 inches down from the top of the longer one to make a lower case "t." All of the notches should be parallel to the ground.

2 Wrap the string around the intersection of the dowels several times, making an "X." Then pull the string up to the top notch, and then thread it through all the other notches, moving in a clockwise direction. Repeat this three times, then make another "X" at the intersection and tie it off.

3 Cut the plastic bag open and lay it flat on the ground, then lay your kite frame on top of the plastic. Cut the plastic so it's about 2 inches bigger than your frame. Fold the plastic over the frame, taping it in place as tight as possible.

Supplies

* 1/4-inch diameter wooden dowel, 33 inches long (it's important that the dowels have some flexibility)
* 1/4-inch diameter wooden dowel, 25 inches long
* heavy-duty, stretchy plastic trash bag
* light-weight packing tape
* scissors
* utility knife
* kite string
* approximately 2 yards of ribbon

*Caution:** Use only with an adult's permission and help.

4 Cut a piece of string about 24 inches long. Tie one end of this string to the long dowel about 5 inches from the top, and wrap the other end to the long dowel about 10 inches from the bottom. Secure both the ends with tape.

5 Tie the kite string about two-thirds of the way up from the bottom, then attach the ribbon to the bottom of the kite. Now you're ready to fly! Just be sure to avoid all overhead lines and—unlike Ben Franklin—don't fly your kite during bad weather!

Note: If your kite spins, add more ribbon to make the tail longer.

 **Time needed:**

45 minutes

Contrary to what many people believe,
Ben's kite was probably not hit by lightning. Even Ben knew
it was too dangerous to fly a kite directly into storm clouds!
It's more likely the kite simply collected enough static
electricity from the nearby clouds
to produce the jolt.

The Union Fire Company and The Pennsylvania Hospital

Ben Franklin began each day by asking, "What good shall I do today?" And he did all kinds of good things that benefited humankind. Aside from his many useful inventions (such as bifocals and the lightning rod), Ben was committed to helping his community.

Two of the many community projects Ben had a significant role in were the first volunteer fire department and the first public hospital in the country.

Because many homes and businesses were made of wood, fires were a problem in colonial times. Ben wanted to help, so he did what he always did when he wanted to bring about change—he wrote about it! Inspired by the organized fire companies he had seen while living in London, Ben wrote an article about the various causes of fires and ways to prevent them. Many people liked the article and took it very seriously. In his autobiography, Ben wrote about how this article "gave rise to a project . . . of forming a company for the more ready extinguishing of fires and mutual assistance in removing and securing of goods when in danger."

An Ounce of Prevention...

In the article that inspired the first fire department, Ben exclaimed, "An ounce of prevention is worth a pound in cure." To prevent fires Ben suggested removing wood from around fireplaces and having the chimney swept regularly. For safety and putting out fires he suggested that homes have water buckets on hand.

Established in 1736, this fire company was called the Union Fire Company, and it had about 30 volunteer members. These men agreed to meet each month to discuss better ways to fight fire and to practice firefighting techniques. (While they were serious about fighting fire, they had some fun sharing stories, too!) They also had buckets and **salvage sacks** on hand at all times. Salvage sacks were bags people used to quickly collect goods if a fire got out of control. Naturally, the group elected Ben as its "Chief."

Ben was delighted by an overwhelming response to the Union Fire Company from the community. After it had formed, so many men continued to volunteer that a handful of other fire companies formed. The **dues** from these groups were used to buy each club a horse-drawn fire engine and other necessary equipment like hooks and ladders. As a result, Philadelphia was well protected from fires. Ben boasted in his autobiography, "since these institutions, the city has never lost by fire more than one or two houses at a time, and the flames have often been extinguished before the house in which they began has been half consumed."

In 1752, Ben further advanced firefighting by founding a fire insurance company called the Philadelphia Contributionship

The first Fire Station in America.

for the Insurance of Houses from Loss by Fire. Folks who were insured by this company had special, lead plaques called fire marks. **Fire marks** were placed on the outside of a building or home to show they were insured, and therefore fire fighters often took greater care in saving those homes or businesses. The Philadelphia Contributionship is still in existence today.

Around the same time he founded the first volunteer fire department, Ben Franklin helped establish the country's first public hospital. Though some colonists (and eventually, historians) credited Ben with the idea, Ben said the idea belonged to his long-time friend Dr. Thomas Bond. Dr. Bond wanted to create a place where Philadelphia's poor could go for medical care. Ben thought this was a great idea and helped by starting a **petition** and writing about the benefits of a public hospital in his newspaper. When Dr. Bond had trouble coming up with the money to build the hospital, Ben stepped in to help with that as well.

Ben asked the Pennsylvania Assembly if they would contribute 2,000 pounds (which was a lot of money) to the hospital if he and Dr. Bond raised that amount on their own. The Assembly agreed, thinking that there was no way two people could raise that much. When Ben and Dr. Bond came through with 2,000 pounds, the Assembly had no choice but to honor their promise or look bad! Ben was tickled by this success. All along Ben knew that he would raise the 2,000 pounds, but he didn't say this to the Assembly. In his autobiog-

Fire bucket.

Ben liked to take what he called "air baths." In other words, he sat naked in his bathtub and let the cold air from an open window clean away any germs!

Another Ounce of Prevention

Ben was a big believer in healthy lifestyles. He recommended exercise, fresh air, and regular bathing. Because his son Francis (Franky) died from **smallpox** at age four, he became a proponent of **inoculations** as well. Many years later, Ben wrote in his autobiography that one of his most bitter regrets in life was that he did not have Franky inoculated against smallpox. An inoculation (or vaccination) put a tiny amount of a disease in a person's body—enough that their body would react and produce immunities, but not so much that it hurt the person. He encouraged other parents not to make the same mistake.

raphy he wrote "I do not remember any of my political maneuvers, the success of which gave me at the time more pleasure, or wherein, after thinking of it, I more readily excused myself for having made some use of cunning."

The Pennsylvania Hospital was founded in 1751 and the building completed in 1755. Before construction was complete, the hospital was housed at the home of the widow of John Kinsey, the Speaker the Assembly. Ben himself wrote the inscription for the cornerstone, which, in part, reads: "This building by the bounty of the government and of many private persons was piously founded for the relief of the sick and miserable"

Words to Know

salvage sacks: bags used to collect valuables quickly during a fire.

dues: money members pay to be a part of a club or organization.

fire marks: plaques used to show a home or business had fire insurance.

petition: a collection of signatures that serves as a collective request for a specific change.

smallpox: a contagious disease that killed a lot people before a vaccination for it was invented. Even though the vaccine was not perfected until 1796, after Ben Franklin died, a form of inoculation against smallpox was practiced in his time.

inoculation: a shot given to protect people from a certain disease or illness.

The original Pennsylvania Hospital building still exists!

Fun Ideas to Try

Form your own bucket brigade, and have a race with another brigade to see who can fill a tub or small pool faster.

Visit a local firehouse or fire museum.

Ben Franklin lost a son to smallpox. Today, smallpox is not a problem in most of the world. Make a list of other diseases that are no longer a problem because of vaccinations.

Create a fire prevention poster or pamphlet.

Ben's fire company was the first volunteer fire department. See if you can find where and when the first paid fire company was established. (Hint: it was before the Union Fire Company!)

Make Your Own
Fire Bucket

In colonial times, each family had a leather fire bucket in case of fire. They used them in bucket brigades. A bucket brigade is a line of people who pass along buckets of water from a water source to the site of a fire. Bucket brigades were necessary in colonial times since fire hydrants weren't invented until the end of the 1700s.

1 Cut off the top third of the plastic bottle with scissors. You might have to ask an adult to help you do this or get you started. You can throw the top piece away. The bottom piece will be your bucket.

2 Wrap the "bucket" in duct tape. Make sure you put tape on the bottom of the bucket, too. Spray paint your bucket following the directions of the paint can and let it dry completely.

3 When the paint is dry, carefully poke 2 holes in the top of the bucket, one on each side. Thread your rope into the holes and tie knots at the ends to make a handle.

4 Now, you're ready to use your bucket! Just fill it with a faucet or hose. You can dip the bucket in water to fill it, too, but the duct tape and paint will come off sooner if you do it this way.

Variation: Instead of covering your bucket with duct tape, you can glue a piece of chamois cloth or a piece of leather around it. These materials can be found at any fabric store. Chamois cloth can usually be found with car washing supplies, too. If you make your bucket this way, you won't be able to dip it in water to fill it.

Supplies
* 2-liter plastic bottle
* scissors
* duct tape
* brown spray paint
* 12-inch piece of rope

Time needed:
30 minutes, not including drying time

Make Your Own
Fire Mark

Fire marks were special plaques that homes and businesses used to show they had fire insurance. They usually had a symbol of some sort, for example, clasping hands or a fire helmet, and the year.

1 Cut the cereal box so that you have at least one good-sized piece of cardboard to make your plaque. You can cut your plaque into whatever shape you'd like. The rest of the box will be used to make the design.

2 Decide on the design you want on your fire mark. Some ideas: a flame, a hydrant, a fire helmet, a fire bucket. Next, sketch your design on a piece of the cardboard. When you're happy with it, cut it out.

3 Sketch the numerals of the year on a piece of cardboard, and cut the numerals out. Arrange your design and the "year" on your plaque, and glue them on.

4 Wrap the plaque with foil and glue it down in the back. Roll the rolling pin over the plaque until the foil is smooth. Your design and the year will be slightly raised.

5 Paint the plaque and let it dry. When the paint is dry, use a steel wool pad to gently rub away some of the paint. This will give your plaque an iron or metallic look.

Supplies

* an empty cereal box or 2 pieces of thin cardboard
* scissors
* pencil
* glue
* foil
* rolling pin
* black tempera paint
* steel wool pad

Time needed:
30 minutes, not including drying time

Make Your Own
Feel-Better Bubble Bath

Ben Franklin was famous for taking "air baths." Ben suspected illnesses were spread from person to person and therefore fresh air could help get rid of illness that was hanging around. Scientists didn't know about germs yet. Here's how to make a bubble bath that can help you feel better if you catch a cold from someone!

1 Add the grated castile soap to the water and stir until the soap is completely dissolved. If you warm the water up in the microwave first, the soap will dissolve faster. Make sure the water doesn't boil, though, and be very careful not to splash the hot water when you start adding ingredients.

2 Stir in the glycerin and the eucalyptus, spearmint, and peppermint oils. Add a few drops of food coloring if you'd like.

3 Pour the mixture into your plastic bottle. The next time you take a bath, add a few capfuls of your bubble bath to the water! The oils will help clear your congestion.

Supplies

* bowl
* 2 cups of distilled water
* 2 ounces of castile soap, grated
* 1 ounce of liquid glycerin from a drug store or craft store
* 3 drops of eucalyptus oil from a crafts store
* 1 or 2 drops of spearmint oil
* 1 or 2 drops of peppermint oil
* a few drops of food coloring
* spoon
* plastic bottle with a lid, like a 20-ounce soda pop bottle

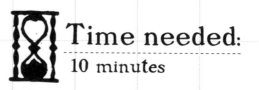

Time needed:
10 minutes

The University of Pennsylvania, Street Improvements, and Daylight Savings Time

s a young boy, Ben had only two years of formal education. Still, as a successful businessman and community leader, Ben felt it was important that boys receive a good education. He wrote about his vision for public school in a pamphlet called "Proposals Relating to the Education of Youth in Pennsylvania."

In this pamphlet, Ben talked about his dream for a school that was **tuition**-free, in a house with lots of land for beauty, room to exercise, plenty of resources, and good teachers who taught things like history, accounting, and writing. In short, Ben wanted the school to teach "everything that is useful." This wasn't surprising considering Ben was the author of *Poor Richard's Almanac*, a book loaded with practical advice and useful information!

Shortly after Ben's pamphlet was published, he stopped dreaming about his school and started raising the money to build it. Ben's vision became a reality when, in 1751, The Philadelphia Academy and Charitable School opened. The students, all boys, ranged in age from 8 to 16. The Academy grew and thrived

The Philadelphia Academy and Charitable School before it became the University of Pennsylvania.

until 1779 when the state Assembly accused the school of being too pro-British, took it over, and renamed it the **University** of Pennsylvania.

Aside from the terrific school he founded, Ben helped improve his beloved city of Philadelphia by improving the streets.

Ben loved the streets of Philadelphia. In his autobiography, he wrote that they were "laid out with a beautiful regularity . . ." But he also noted that "in wet weather the wheels of heavy **carriages** ploughed them into a quagmire, so that it was difficult to cross them, and in dry weather the dust was offensive." As usual, Ben talked and wrote about the subject until the people running the city were convinced to pave the main market streets with bricks. The paved streets did a great deal to improve carriage travel as well as foot traffic. People didn't have to climb over steep or muddy ruts to cross the street. But soon, there was another problem. The paved streets were often dirty. To

Dr. Franklin

After his invention of the lightning rod and his groundbreaking work with electricity, Ben had become a famous and respected scientist. As such, he received many awards and honorary degrees from some very prestigious schools, including Harvard and Yale. An honorary degree is a special way to honor or celebrate the achievements of someone who did not actually attend the school. In 1759, while on a trip to Scotland, Ben was awarded an honorary doctorate from the University of St. Andrews. Two years later, he received another honorary doctorate from Oxford University. Ben was very proud of his honorary doctorates. He liked to be called Dr. Franklin.

Daylight Savings Time

Streetlamps weren't the only light issue that Ben investigated. At age 78, while living in France, Ben wrote an essay titled "An Economical Project." This essay had ideas about how people could better use sunlight and save resources like candles and lamp oil. Some of his ideas, like ringing church bells or firing cannons to make sure everyone got up at sunrise, sounded pretty crazy. It's hard to know if Ben was being serious or not. What Ben was really getting at was what we know as **Daylight Savings Time!** Ben was an early advocate of taking advantage of the extra summer daylight. Today we change the clocks in the summer for just this reason. This practice was used in some places in the world during World War I, and officially adopted in the United Sates in 1918.

solve this problem, Ben convinced shop owners to keep brooms and hire workers to sweep up the streets in front of their shops. The whole plan worked out very well. Ben wrote, "All the inhabitants of the city were delighted with the cleanliness of the pavement that surrounded the market, it being a con-

venience to all, and this raised a general desire to have all the streets paved, and made the people more willing to submit to a tax for that purpose."

In addition to getting the streets paved, Ben improved the design of the city's streetlamps. Ben credits a man named John Clifton for inspiring shop owners to help light the streets by putting out a lamp by each shop. The original

The immaculate streets of Philadelphia.

Words to Know

tuition: the money paid to attend a privately owned school.

university: a group of colleges or a school of higher education.

carriages: horse-drawn vehicles used in colonial times.

Daylight Savings Time: the time of the year when clocks are set ahead, usually one hour, so that people can enjoy more daylight.

streetlamps were globe-shaped. The problem with them was that no air circulated inside them and this caused smoke to fill up the globe and block the light. If one got accidentally hit or bumped, the entire globe would break. Ben suggested the new lamps be made with "four flat planes, with a long funnel . . . to draw up the smoke." This way, Ben argued, the lamps would provide more light, be easier to clean (because there would be less smoke inside), and be easily repaired since only broken panels would have to be replaced.

A Family Affair

Ben Franklin had eight grandchildren. He took two of them under his wing, sometimes inviting them to travel with him and supporting their educations. These two grandsons were Temple Franklin (William's son) and Benjamin Franklin Bache, who was called Benny. (Benny was Sally's son.) Benny Bache went to the University of Pennsylvania and later became a printer just like his grandfather. Of course, Ben loved his other six grandchildren very much, too. They belonged to Sally and her husband Richard, and their names were William, Louis, Elizabeth, Deborah, Sarah, and Richard. When Ben lived with Sally and her family as an old man, he loved being in his grandkids' company. He wrote that they "afford me great pleasure."

Make Your Own
Paving Brick

1 Pinch the milk cartoon closed and tape it shut. Next, fold the top down so that the carton has a squared-off top (instead of a pointy one). Tape the top to the sides.

2 Lay the milk carton on its side and carefully cut off the top two thirds. When you're done, you should have a rectangular mold that's a couple of inches tall.

3 Prepare the plaster of paris according to the directions on the package. Add the paint until you get the desired brick color and stir.

4 Pour the plaster into the mold and let it set. This process will go faster if you set the brick outside in the sun.

5 If you'd like, you can press decorative stones into the brick or use an unfolded paper clip to etch your name or a design into the plaster before it dries completely.

6 When the plaster is dry, carefully peel away the milk carton.

Supplies

* rectangular, half-gallon milk or juice carton, cleaned and dried
* duct tape
* scissors
* plaster of paris
* brick-red craft paint made by mixing red and brown paint
* stirring stick
* paper clip, glass pebbles, or decorative stones (optional)

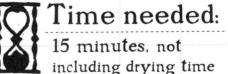

Time needed:

15 minutes, not including drying time

Make Your Own
Street Lamp

1 Take the lid off the shoebox. Cut a large rectangle out of each side as well as out of the lid. These will be the openings for your lamp.

2 Paint the inside and the outside of the box and lid with the black paint. Let the paint dry.

3 Cut four pieces of plastic wrap that are slightly larger than the four openings you made in the sides of the box. Carefully tape the pieces of plastic wrap to the inside of the box and lid. These will be your "glass" panels.

4 In one of the ends of the box, carefully cut a circle that's big enough for the handle of the flashlight to slide through. Slide it through the hole until the top of the flashlight rests against the opening in the box. Put the lid back on the box. You can secure the flashlight with some tape. Turn the box so the flashlight's handle hangs down toward the ground.

5 Hang your street lamp using a piece of yarn threaded through two holes in the top, at the end opposite the flashlight. You can also use a few pieces of Tack Putty on one of the long sides of the box to attach your street lamp to a wall.

6 Turn on your flashlight and turn off the lights. Now the room will be lit up colonial style!

The street lamps used in colonial times used candles.

Supplies

* shoebox with a lid
* scissors
* black paint
* clear, plastic wrap or four sheets of laminating paper from any office supply store
* masking tape, yarn
* flashlight

Time needed:
20 minutes, not including drying time

Postal Service

With no telephones or computers, colonists communicated the only way they could—with letters. Unfortunately, the colonial mail system wasn't very good. Sometimes delivery took many weeks—even by boat, which was considered the fastest way to send mail. Sometimes mail was stolen or simply lost. On top of this, there were no official post offices. Mail was handed out at **inns** or **taverns** or other gathering places. The fact that the 13 colonies all had different rules and ways of doing things only made the whole system worse. There was no unity! But Ben Franklin changed that.

In 1753, England's king, King George III, made Ben a Deputy Postmaster of the 13 colonies. Ben shared the job with a man named William Hunter. One of the first things Ben did was travel the **postal routes** and talk to all the postal workers. The trip covered about 1,700 miles! He wanted to see if the postal

Before being appointed postmaster for the 13 colonies, the British Crown appointed Ben postmaster of Philadelphia. This happened in 1737.

workers had any ideas about how to improve things. With their help, Ben reformed the system into a well-organized and profitable business within four years.

One important improvement was to maintain the postal routes. Before Ben had the markings of the routes improved, mail carriers sometimes got lost. So it took them longer to deliver the mail. Ben also made the mail routes more direct, so that the distance between major locations was as short as could be. How did Ben shorten the distance between locations? He measured them with the **odometer** he invented. Ben attached his odometer to the wheel of his wagon. It worked by keeping track of the number of rotations the wheel made over a journey. The odometer in a car keeps track of the miles a car travels, and it works in a similar way.

Ben writing down ideas on reforming the postal system.

Words to Know

inn: a place where travelers can spend the night, eat, rest, or visit.

tavern: a place where people can buy food and drink and enjoy each other's company.

postal route: a path taken by mail carriers to deliver the mail.

odometer: a device used to measure distances traveled by a vehicle.

Franking Privilege: the special right that elected officials have to send

official mail through the postal system free of charge by simply signing their names in place of a postage stamp.

Continental Congress: the group of delegates from the rebel colonies who met during and after the American Revolution. They issued the Declaration of Independence and the Articles of Confederation.

phonetic: spelling that reflects just how words sound.

The **Franking Privilege** is a special right or perk that elected officials enjoy. It allows them to send official mail through the postal system for free. The word "franking" comes from the Latin word "francus," which means "free." To use this privilege, an official just signs his or her name where a stamp should go. Ben Franklin had an unusual franking signature. It read: B. Free Franklin. Many believe this was Ben's clever way of showing his support for America's independence from England.

Ben made other significant improvements. For example, he had postal workers keep detailed records of mail delivery. He also had newspapers publish the names of folks who had mail that needed to be picked up for mail carriers to see. To speed up delivery times he had mail wagons travel during the night instead of just during the day. To deal with all the undeliverable mail, he created a special post office to send it to. This first "dead letter" office was in Philadelphia. In addition, Ben created a rate chart for postmasters across the colonies to use. This chart, like the rate system today, calculated postage based on weight and distance.

Ben's odometer.

Ben remained postmaster for the 13 colonies until 1774, when he was fired by the British government for being a vocal supporter of America's independence from England. In 1775, though, the **Continental Congress** appointed Ben Postmaster for the United Colonies. He resigned after a year to become an ambassador to France.

Ben Franklin is often called the Father of the United States Postal System.

Ben's improvements to the postal system were more important than just people getting their letters more quickly. Once there was an effective means to communicate, the 13 colonies began to see how they could work together.

Dear Congress

Ben Franklin loved to write letters! He spent his whole life writing letters to friends, family members, colleagues, and his fellow colonists. Everyone enjoyed Ben's letters. Folks often passed them around to share and newspapers frequently printed them. Many of Ben's letters are preserved in libraries and books for us to read. One of these letters, dated February 3, 1790, is the one Ben wrote to Congress making a case to abolish slavery in the United States. Ben had owned slaves and allowed "Slave for sale" ads in his newspaper, but he changed his position on slavery later in life. He became president of the Pennsylvania Society for Promoting the Abolition of Slavery in 1787. Because he was so well respected, Ben's words inspired Congress to publicly debate the slavery issue for the first time.

Before there were postage stamps, people paid for their mail when they picked it up.

This was really the beginning of America's independence. To honor all that he did for the postal system, the United States Postal Service put Ben Franklin's portrait on one of the first two United States postage stamps. Ben's stamp was worth 5 cents. The other stamp, worth 10 cents, featured George Washington. These stamps were issued on July 1, 1847.

Ben's actual handwriting.

Ben once created a phonetic alphabet. This alphabet got rid of the letters that Ben thought weren't needed, and it added new ones. He tried using this alphabet for a time but gave it up once it was clear no one else liked it.

Make Your Own
Personal Mailbox

When you're done with this mailbox, you can hang it by your bedroom door, on a desk, or wherever you'd like.

1 Cut about 2 inches of the lid's plastic lip off. In that 2-inch space, use a piece of tape to secure the lid to the container. The tape will act as a hinge so that the lid can "open" or "close."

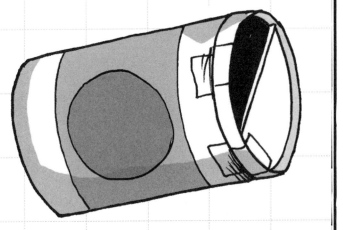

2 Cover the oatmeal container with white construction paper. Cover the end of the container and the top of the lid with two circles of white construction paper.

3 Cut a small flag out of the cardboard. Use the marker to color the flag red.

4 Turn the container so it's horizontal. Place the flag vertically on one side of the container about half way down and half way across. Pole a small hole in the side and attach the flag to the mailbox using the brad. Your flag should move up and down, like a real mailbox flag.

Supplies

* empty oatmeal container with a lid or a similar cardboard cylinder
* masking tape or duct tape
* scissors
* white construction paper
* red marker
* piece of thin cardboard
* one paper brad
* glue
* various markers, glitter, or stickers for decorating
* piece of ribbon or rope

5 Keeping your container horizontal, use the scissors to carefully poke two holes in the top of the mailbox. (Ask an adult to help!) Put one hole at the end of the mailbox and the other hole near the lid. Push your ribbon through the holes and tie knots at the end. You can use the ribbon to hang up your mailbox, and you can decorate your mailbox however you'd like! Don't forget to write your name somewhere so people can deliver your mail.

Time needed:
25 minutes

Make Your Own
Mail Bag

1 Sew or glue a 1-inch hem at the top and bottom of your material. Lay the material on your work area so that the front side of the material is facing down. You want the "back side" of the material to face you.

2 Fold the bottom up 12 inches. Then fold the top piece down to make a flap. The front side of the material should now be showing.

3 Turn the material over. Make a mark about an inch from the sides where the ends of the handle should go. When you're done, open the folded material again.

5 Cut your nylon webbing to the desired handle length. Dab some Fray Check or a thin line of hot glue on the ends to keep them from unraveling.

6 Attach the handle ends on the marks you made on the material.

7 Lay the material down so that the inside of the fabric is facing down. The outside of the fabric should be facing you.

8 Fold the bottom up 12 inches. Move the handle so it's out of the way.

9 Sew a ½-inch hem on both sides of the material.

10 Turn the bag inside out. Fold the flap down and now you're ready to decorate and then deliver mail or carry some books!

Time needed:
25 minutes

Supplies

* ❋ sewing machine OR a hot glue gun*
* ❋ sturdy material such as canvas, denim, or oilcloth, 13 inches wide by 36 inches long**
* ❋ 1 yard of nylon webbing, 1 to 2 inches wide
* ❋ Fray Check™ or a bit of hot glue
* ❋ scissors
* ❋ ruler or tape measure
* ❋ fabric paint (optional)

*Use only with an adult's permission and help

** If you use oilcloth, you will need a heavy-duty needle in your sewing machine

Fun Ideas to Try

Ben Franklin had a unique Franking Signature. Create a special one of your own. What do you want your signature to say about you?

Late in life, Ben took a stand against slavery. One thing he did was write a petition. Write a petition for a cause you believe in.

Take a tour of a local post office.

Invite a stamp collector to show you his or her collection.

Ben created a phonetic alphabet. Make up your own alphabet or secret code and write a friend a letter using it.

Learn about the Pony Express, the route mail carriers took from Missouri to California during the Wild West times.

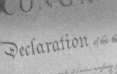

The Declaration of Independence

nlike many people, Ben Franklin did not spend his retirement years sitting around. He played a large role in the founding of a new country—the United States of America.

Before the American colonies declared their independence, they were governed by England. In 1756, France and England began to fight for control over the colonies and the territories in the New World. Because each side had its own Native American allies, this war is called the **French and Indian War**. It is also called the **Seven Year's War** because it lasted seven years. England won, but the government had to borrow a lot of money for the war that had to be repaid. England's king felt that the colonists should help with this expence, as well as for the British troops that were left behind to protect them. And so in 1765, Parliament passed the Stamp Act.

The Stamp Act said colonists who bought paper products had to pay for a special tax label or stamp. The stamp was required on all kinds of paper goods, including calendars, newspapers, advertisements, legal contracts like wills and marriage licenses, and even decks of cards! The colonists, of course, were very upset with the Stamp Act. No one likes taxes. But they were especially upset because they had no say in their government, no say in the laws and taxes imposed on them. The British Parliament was one of the branches of British government that came up with the Stamp Act, and they were 3,000 miles away. The colonists declared that this was "taxation without representation." Ben Franklin called the Stamp Act "the mother of mischief." At the request of leaders within the colonies, Ben traveled to England to speak on their behalf. Ben presented the case very well, and shortly after his presentation, the Stamp Act was **repealed**.

The Boston Tea Party.

Words to Know

French and Indian War: the war between the British and French over territory in America.

Seven Year's War: another name for the French and Indian War.

repeal: to cancel or take back a law.

boycott: refusing to buy things in protest.

riot: public violence or disorder in protest or response to something.

Boston Massacre: a riot in Boston that resulted in five colonists being shot and killed by British troops.

Trouble between England and the colonies was far from over though. In fact, it was just beginning. In 1767, Parliament passed the Townsend Acts. This imposed heavy taxes on lots of products, including paper and tea, that the colonists bought from England. The colonists responded by **boycotting** all products made in England. Ben was still in London trying to ease tensions between America and England. He thought the boycott was a good idea even though he realized things were bound to get worse. When colonists **rioted** in response to the Townsend Acts, England sent military troops to deal with the unruly colonists. Ben called it a "dangerous step."

Finally, in 1770, Parliament repealed most of the Townsend Acts. They only left the duty on one product. That product was tea. Colonists rioted even more. One of these riots, known as the **Boston Massacre**, resulted in five colonists being shot and killed by British troops for throwing snowballs and yelling at them.

Tension between the colonists and England continued to grow. In 1773, England passed the Tea Act. This made it illegal for colonists to buy tea from anyone but a British-owned company. Angry colonists reacted by boycotting tea and then by dressing up as Indians, boarding three English tea ships in Boston Harbor and dumping over 300 chests of tea overboard. The "Boston Tea Party" made Ben sad. He wrote: "I am at a loss to see how peace and union are to be restored."

To get back at the colonists for the Boston Tea Party, Parliament passed a series of laws in 1774. The British called these laws the Coercive Acts. The colonists called them the Intolerable Acts. These laws led to more trouble. They required the colonists to close Boston Harbor until the tea, and the tax

The Battle of Lexington.

on the tea, was paid for. The colonies responded by sending **delegates** to a meeting in Philadelphia to decide what to do next. Georgia was the only colony of the 13 not to send a delegate. This meeting was called the First Continental Congress. Around the time when the First Continental Congress met, Ben was still living in England, and he continued to fully support the colonists. In a letter he wrote shortly before leaving England he said it wasn't only the colonists' rights and freedoms at stake, but that of "endless generations" of Americans.

In 1775, after Ben had decided there was nothing more he could do in England, he returned to America. At the time of his journey, the war had not yet begun, but tensions had been running high for a long time. In April of that year, a group of British soldiers was ordered to march from Boston to Concord, Massachusetts, because British military leaders had heard colonists were storing gunpowder and weapons there. They wanted to surprise the colonists and

Words to Know

delegate: a person chosen or elected by a group to represent them at a meeting.

redcoats: the nickname given by colonists to the British troops because they wore red coats.

Minutemen: colonists who fought for independence from England.

Battle of Lexington: the fight between Minutemen and redcoats that officially began the Revolutionary War.

loyalist: an American colonist who believed America should stay under England's rule.

Revolutionary War: the war of independence fought between America and England.

Family Affair

In 1772, Ben's wife, Deborah, pleaded with him to come home. Her health was poor and she feared she'd never see Ben again. Ben was in England at the time, trying to ease tensions between the colonies and the British. Whatever the reasons were, Ben didn't return home until 1775, a year after Deborah had died. The fact that Ben missed her funeral made his son William very angry. Unfortunately, the bad feelings between Will and Ben had already existed for some time before the funeral and continued throughout the rest of Ben's life. One of the reasons was that Will was a **loyalist** who remained loyal to the British, and Ben, of course, was a firm believer in America's independence. This was a common source of disagreement within families.

catch them red-handed with the weapons. But, late at night, a man named Paul Revere rode ahead of the British soldiers and warned the colonists that the **redcoats** were coming. Just outside the town of Lexington, redcoats and volunteer colonial soldiers called **Minutemen** faced off in a battle known as the **Battle of Lexington**. After killing eight colonists, the British soldiers marched on to Concord. There, hundreds of Minutemen were ready for them. That was the beginning of the **Revolutionary War**.

On May 6, 1775, the delegates from the colonies came together once again to try to figure out how to proceed. This was called the Second Continental Congress. At age 69, Ben Franklin was the oldest of all the delegates, but he worked harder than anyone to promote the need for independence. He also worked hard to support the Revolutionary War. He organized a new postal system because after the war

(from right to left) Ben Franklin, John Adams, Thomas Jefferson, Robert Livingston, and Roger Sherman discussing the Declaration of Independence.

began the British postal system in the colonies was abolished. And he helped General George Washington organize the American soldiers and resources.

Despite poor treatment from England, many colonists struggled to decide whether to join the war for independence or to stay loyal to England. But in January 1776, a writer and friend of Ben's named Thomas Paine wrote an essay called "Common Sense." The essay, published by Ben, was highly critical of England and helped convince many undecided colonists to join the fight for independence. Within months, most members of the Second Continental Congress had begun to see the need for full independence, too. In June 1776, the group asked Ben Franklin, along with Thomas Jefferson, John Adams, Robert Livingston, and Roger Sherman, to write a formal declaration of independence.

Words to Know

Declaration of Independence: the document written by Thomas Jefferson, declaring the independence of the United States.
treason: actions or words that go against one's own country.
parchment: the skin of a sheep or goat prepared for writing.

Declaration of Independence.

Though Ben was the most accomplished writer of the group, the five men chose Thomas Jefferson to put the Declaration to paper. Ben had been ill and, knowing how unselfish he was, he probably didn't mind. After Jefferson wrote the Declaration, he sent it to Ben to edit. Ben suggested only minor changes, but one of them is famous. Originally Jefferson had written, "We hold these truths to be sacred and un-

---

Ben Franklin wanted the turkey to be the national bird, not the eagle. He thought the eagle was "a bird of bad moral character" and that the turkey was "a respectable bird, and a true, original native of America."

Unity

Ben created the first political cartoon involving the colonies in 1754. It was a drawing of a snake cut into pieces. Each piece was labeled with an abbreviation for the names of the colonies, and under the snake were the words: Join, or Die. The cartoon was meant to convince colonists to join the fight during the French and Indian War. He printed it again during the Revolutionary War to convince the colonists to stand up to England.

deniable . . ." Ben changed this phrase to "We hold these truths to be self-evident." (The whole line reads: We hold these truths to be self-evident that all men are created equal.)

On July 4, 1776, after some debate, the Second Continental Congress unanimously approved the **Declaration of Independence**. Supporting the document was considered an act of **treason** by England. Although this could have meant death, 56 brave delegates signed it about a month later.

Most historians believe a second copy of the Declaration was made on sturdier **parchment** and signed in August, and that this is the document we still have today. Signing this document was scary for everyone involved. As the story goes, John Hancock said, "We must be unanimous; there must be no pulling different ways; we must all hang together." Ben replied, "Yes. We must all hang together, or most assuredly, we shall hang separately!"

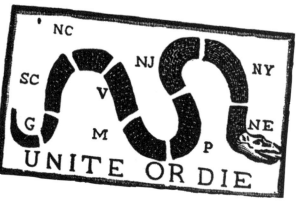

Fun Ideas to Try

Create your own political cartoon.

Ben Franklin said, "in this world nothing can be said to be certain except death and taxes." What do you think he meant by this? Do you think taxes are important? Discuss your answers.

Make Your Own
Parchment Paper

The Declaration of Independence was written on parchment paper. Here's a simple way to make paper that looks like parchment.

1 Carefully rip the edges of your paper. Crumple your piece of paper into a tight ball, then flatten your paper out and lay it on the cookie sheet. This will give your paper an older appearance.

2 Pour the coffee or tea all over the paper and let it soak in for five minutes. Lift the paper up by a corner and let any extra liquid drain off.

3 Carefully lay the piece of paper flat on a towel or out in the sun. You can also speed up the drying process using a blow dryer set on the lowest setting. Just be careful not to burn yourself or the paper.

5 Let the paper dry completely before using markers or pens to write on it. Or better yet, use your feather pen from the following activity. When you're done, roll up the document like a scroll and use the ribbon to tie it up.

Supplies

* ½ cup or so of cold coffee OR tea
* large piece of white paper
* cookie sheet or another shallow tray
* paper towel
* pen or markers
* piece of ribbon

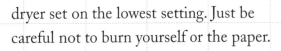

Time needed:
10 minutes, not including drying time

Make Your Own
Feather Pen

Delegate John Hancock was the first person to sign the Declaration of Independence. He's famous for doing so in big letters. He said he wanted King George III to be able to see it all the way in England. His bold way of signing his name came to symbolize anyone writing their signature. Here's a simple-but-fancy pen you can use to write your own "John Hancock" on your parchment paper.

1 Put the tip of the feather about two inches from the tip of the pen.

2 Use a small piece of masking tape to secure the feather to the pen.

Time needed:
5 minutes

Supplies
* 1 large feather from any craft store
* ballpoint pen
* masking tape

Make Your Own
Liberty Bell

The Declaration of Independence was read to the public for the first time on July 8, 1776. This took place in Pennsylvania's statehouse yard. According to a popular version of the story, people were called to the gathering by the ringing of the Liberty Bell. Many historians don't believe the Liberty Bell was rung on that day because there is written evidence that the bell's steeple was in need of repair at the time.

1 Turn the cup upside down and carefully tear a small crack beginning at the lip of the cup.

2 Cover the entire cup with foil. Make a little tear in the foil over the top of the tear in the cup.

3 If you want to, you can make the bottom of the cup look more bell-shaped by gently rolling up the edges of the cup or by adding more foil to the bottom and shaping it.

4 Poke one end of the pipe cleaner in one side of the cup, about 1 inch from the top. Once the pipe cleaner is inside the cup, string the jingle bell onto the end.

5 Poke the pipe cleaner through the other side of the bell. Your jingle bell is on the inside. Twist the ends of the pipe cleaner together.

6 Paint the foil with a coat of gray paint. Don't worry if all the nooks and crannies of the foil aren't painted. You don't want it to be perfect; you want it to have a weathered look. Let the paint dry. Even though the real Liberty Bell (which has an E-Flat tone) hasn't been rung since 1846, your bell should ring nicely!

Supplies

* large paper cup—preferably not Styrofoam because it won't work quite as well
* foil
* 1 black pipe cleaner
* 1 medium-sized jingle bell
* gray craft paint

Time needed:

20 minutes, not including drying time

Fun Ideas to Try

The Liberty Bell cracked and was repaired a few times before the last, unrepairable crack in the Liberty Bell was made. Nobody knows how it cracked. Write a funny tale that tells the story of how it happened.

Read a copy of the Declaration of Independence.

Pretend you are a writer from 1788 and write a newspaper story about the election of George Washington as President. Be sure to include biographical information about the country's first president.

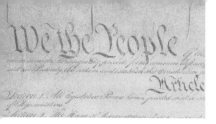

The Constitution of the United States and the Treaty of Alliance

The Declaration of Independence was a great moment in the history of the United States of America. But it did not end the Revolutionary War. England still did not recognize America as an independent country and continued to battle for control of the colonies.

The founding fathers knew that America needed help to win. They asked Ben to go to France and ask for support. In December 1776, at age 71, Ben got on a ship headed for France. His grandsons Temple (who was 17) and Benny (who was 7) went with him. The people of France loved Ben; they had his image put on all kinds of things such as medals and rings. This amused Ben. In a letter to his daughter Sally, he wrote, "My face is as well known as that of the moon!" Ben enjoyed his life in France. He lived in a fancy home and had many friends. He also fell in love again with a woman named Madame Anne-Catherine Helvetius.

Ben proposed to Anne-Catherine but she turned him down in memory of her late husband.

For nearly two years, Ben worked to convince the French to help America. All the while he had to be careful because he knew there were British spies trying to find out what he was up to in France and who he was talking to. Ben's butler was even believed by some to be a spy.

During the early part of the war, the news Ben heard from home was usually not good. British troops were dominating the Americans. In 1777, Ben was extremely disturbed to hear that the British had taken control of his beloved home city, Philadelphia.

Over time, the news from the colonies improved. One fateful day word reached France that American soldiers had defeated the British in a big skirmish called the Battle of Saratoga. General Horatio Gates and his troops, on the American side, captured an important British general and his whole army. General Burgoyne was the commander who had taken Philadelphia. This victory helped show France that America was strong and would make a good **ally**.

On February 6, 1778, Ben and French officials signed the **Treaty of Alliance.** With this treaty, France officially recognized America as a country and promised to help them win independence from England. Afterwards, Ben thanked the king, King Louis XVI of France, and pledged America's loyalty to him and his country. In addition to the money France had already loaned America, France sent warships and soldiers.

"It's not possible to repay what I, and every other American, owe . . . France," Ben said.

The Battle of Saratoga.

Discussing America's interests with a gentleman from France.

America fought the final battle of the Revolutionary War, the Battle of Yorktown, with the help of France. This battle took place between October 9 and 19, 1781, and when it was over America was free. Shortly afterward, Congress asked Ben to try to work out peace with England. The task was difficult as there were still a lot of hard feelings between the two countries. In 1783, though, England signed the **Treaty of Paris** (also known as the Paris Peace Treaty.). According to this treaty, England recognized America as an independent country and agreed to pay for some of the damages of the war. In a letter to a friend, Ben wrote: "We are now friends with England and with all mankind. May we never see another war! For in my opinion there was never a good war or a bad peace."

Words to Know

ally: a person or country who shares a common goal.

Treaty of Alliance: a treaty signed by France officially recognizing America as an ally in 1778.

Treaty of Paris: the treaty between England and the newly independent America signed in 1783.

Constitutional Convention: the meeting in Philadelphia that took place between May 25 and September 17, 1787, at which the U.S. Constitution was written.

separation of powers: the purpose of having three different branches of government to make sure that no one group gains more power than the others.

House of Representatives: a part of congress in which the number of representatives is based on a state's population.

Senate: a part of congress where each state is given two representatives.

Constitution of the United States of America: the document that contains the supreme law of the United States.

epitaph: an inscription on a grave that describes or is in memory of the person buried there.

With the war over, Ben bid his friends in France farewell and on September 14, 1785, he returned home to Philadelphia to live out his life. His family—and the whole city—welcomed him home. At age 79, Ben longed to retire from public service. It was not to be. Instead, Pennsylvania leaders asked him to become governor of the state, a position he served for three years. During those years, Ben participated in one last important event—the **Constitutional Convention**.

The signing of the Constitution of the United States.

Constitutional Convention

The delegates to the Constitutional Convention set up America's government with three branches. The Legislative Branch includes the Senate and House of Representatives, and is in charge of creating laws. The Judicial Branch includes the Supreme Court, and is in charge of deciding how to apply laws and to make sure everything goes according to the Constitution. The Executive Branch includes the President and Vice President, and helps make sure laws are carried out. The Executive Branch also conducts foreign affairs. The purpose of having three different branches is to make sure that no one group gains more power than the others. This concept is known as "**separation of powers**."

The original Colonial flag.

The purpose of the Constitutional Convention was to set up a government for the newly established United States of America. Though the delegates agreed on a system of government with three branches, they argued about representation. Representation was an important issue to the delegates— it was part of what they fought for in the Revolutionary War. The states with larger populations felt they deserved more representatives in congress, but the smaller states worried that then they wouldn't have a fair say. Ben helped save the day by endorsing the Great Compromise, which held that there would be a **House of Representatives**, where the number of representatives was based on a state's population, and a **Senate**, where states would each have two representatives. This idea is also referred to as the Connecticut Compromise and was devised by Roger Sherman and Oliver Ellsworth. In June 1788, states voted to adopt this idea as well as the entire **Constitution of the United States of America**. The following April, George Washington was elected the first president of the United States and John Adams was elected vice president.

In the last few years of his long, full life, Ben lived with his daughter Sally and her family. He adored being around his grandkids, and friends like Thomas Jefferson came to visit him. In the spring of 1790, Ben came down with a respiratory infection. And on April 17 of that year, Ben died peacefully

Familiar Signature

Ben Franklin was the only person to sign all four of the documents that made American independence and government possible: the Declaration of Independence, the Treaty of Alliance, the 1783 Treaty of Paris, and the Constitution of the United States.

Franklin's Epitaph

Ben was buried next to his wife, Deborah, and near his son, Francis, in the Christ Church Cemetery. The gravestone has a simple inscription: Benjamin and Deborah Franklin 1790. But when Ben was in his twenties, he wrote his own **epitaph**, which showed his humor and love of books:

The Body of
B. Franklin,
Printer;
Like the Cover of an old Book,
Its Contents torn out,
And stript of its Lettering and Gilding,
Lies here, Food for Worms.
But the Work shall not be wholly lost;
For it will, as he believ'd, appear once more,
In a new & more perfect Edition,
Corrected and amended
By the Author.

Ben Franklin's grave.

at age 84. News of his death spread around the world. People everywhere stopped and remembered the great man whose inventions and scientific discoveries had changed the world and whose unselfishness and charisma had touched so many people and helped create a new nation.

Make Your Own
Fur Hat

In order to help show that Americans were down-to-earth folks, Ben often wore plain clothes and a simple fur hat while in France. The tactic to win approval worked. Some paintings show Ben wearing his famous hat.

1 Wrap the poster board around your forehead to see how long it should be, and mark it at this point.

2 Unroll the poster board and lay it on top of the fake fur. Then cut a piece of fake fur that is the same size as the poster board.

3 Overlap the ends of the poster board slightly and tape them together to make a cylinder. This cylinder should fit securely around your head. If it doesn't, adjust the ends.

4 Spread out the rest of your fake fur with the fur side down. Stand the cylinder up on top of it. About one inch from the edge of the poster board, draw a line around to make a circle. Cut out the circle and glue it on one end of the

poster board cylinder. You should have enough fur to overlap the edge slightly.

5 Glue the rectangular piece of fur around the rest of the cylinder. You can cut the extra length off the end if you don't want the fur to overlap. Once the glue is dried, you can put your hat on and walk around in Ben Franklin style!

Supplies

* piece of poster board 7 inches tall and wide enough to go around your head
* scissors
* ½ yard of fake fur from any fabric or craft store
* masking tape
* glue

Time needed:
30 minutes

Make Your Own
Travel Log

Ben often kept a travel log, or journal, of his travels. This included his final journey to and from France. Here's a simple way to make your own travel log that has pockets for holding photos or other souvenirs of your trips.

1 Glue down the bottom flaps of the lunch bags so the bags lie flat. Cut off about ¼ inch of the closed end of both bags (the end where the flap is.) Lay one bag directly on top of the other.

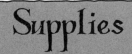

2 Staple the bags together with one staple right in the middle of the bags. The staple should be parallel to the short ends of the bags. If your stapler won't reach the middle of the bags, fold the bags in half, lengthwise, and staple on the edge.

3 Fold the bags along the staple. You should now have a book that is approximately 5 by 5 inches. Punch two holes, one on each side of the staple.

4 Thread short pieces of string through the holes and tie with bows. Now, you're ready to use your travel log! Just write on the pages using a marker or a pen. You can use the "pockets" to store photos or other small items.

Supplies

* paper lunch bags, brown or white
* glue
* scissors
* stapler
* hole puncher
* string or yarn

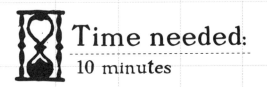

Time needed:
10 minutes

Glossary

A

allies: people, groups, or countries who agree to help each other.

almanac: a reference book containing information, such as weather forecasts, lists and tables, moon phases and tide charts, short articles and household tips.

ambassador: someone who represents his or her country.

American Philosophical Society: a group of men from various colonies who joined together to share information about scientific and mathematical discoveries, new arts and trades, maps and charts, and, in general, ideas for improving life in the colonies.

apprentice: someone who agrees to work for a certain amount of time for a craftsman or professional in return for being taught a trade.

armonica: a musical instrument invented by Ben Franklin in 1761. It is played by rubbing your wet fingers against a set of turning, crystal bowls.

atoms: tiny particles of matter that make up everything.

autobiography: a book that a person writes about his or her life.

B

bartering: a system where people exchange goods or services for other goods or services.

Battle of Lexington: the fight between Minutemen and redcoats in Lexington, Massachusetts, on April 19, 1775 that officially began the Revolutionary War.

Battle of Yorktown: the final battle of the Revolutionary War, which began on October 9, 1781 and ended ten days later.

bifocals: glasses with lenses that are divided into two parts, invented by Ben Franklin in 1784. The upper half is for looking at things far away and the lower half is for reading or for looking at things that are near.

Boston Massacre: a riot in Boston that took place on March 5, 1770 and resulted in five colonists being shot and killed by British Troops.

Boston Tea Party: the December 16, 1773 act of protest against the Tea Act in which a group of colonists disguised themselves as Native Americans, boarded a ship, and dumped British tea into the Boston Harbor.

boycott: the act of not buying a certain product in order to protest something.

C

carriages: horse-drawn vehicles used in colonial times.

circuit: a system of conductors forming a path for electricity to move.

Coercive Acts (or Intolerable Acts): a group of laws imposed in 1774 on the colonists by England as a way to punish them for the Boston Tea Party.

colonies: groups of British settlements in America.

conductor: a material through which electricity moves.

Constitutional Convention: the meeting in Philadelphia that lasted from May 25 to September 17, 1787, at which the U.S. Constitution was created.

Constitution of the United States: the document that lays out the rules and principals of the United States government.

Continental Congress: the group of delegates from rebel communities who met during and after the American Revolution. They issued the Declaration of Independence and the Articles of Confederation.

counterfeit money: fake money.

currency: another name for money, or something of value that can be exchanged for goods.

current: a body of water that is moving in a certain direction.

D

declaration: something announced or declared.

Declaration of Independence: the document written by Thomas Jefferson and edited by Ben Franklin that declares America's independence from England. It was signed on July 4, 1776.

delegate: someone who goes to a meeting to represent his or her city or country.

Daylight Savings Time: the time of the year when clocks are set ahead or held back one hour past standard time so that people can enjoy more daylight.

dues: money members pay to be a part of a club or organization.

E

electricity: energy created by the movement of electrons between atoms.

electrons: particles that, along with protons and the nucleus, make an atom.

electrostatic machine: a machine used to generate sparks of electricity.

engraving: a type of printing in which the design is etched or drawn into the plate instead of having the letters or design raised on the plate.

epitaph: an inscription on a grave that describes or is in memory of the person buried there.

F

fire companies: groups organized to fight fires.

fire marks: plaques used to show that a home or business had fire insurance.

First Continental Congress: a group of delegates from the colonies who met to discuss what to do about England's Coercive Acts (or Intolerable Acts) in 1774.

Franking Privilege: a special right given to elected officials, allowing them to send official mail through the postal system free of charge by signing their names in place of a postage stamp.

Franklin/Folger Map: the Gulf Stream map Ben Franklin and his whaling cousin Timothy Folger created in 1786.

French and Indian War or The Seven Year's War: the war between France and England and their Native American allies for control over the colonies in America. It lasted from 1756 to 1763.

frugal: careful not to waste money or resources.

G

government: the group of people who lead a city or country.

Gregorian calendar: a calendar introduced in 1582 by Pope Gregory XIII to revise the Julian calendar to bring it back into synchronization with the seasons. It was adopted in Great Britain and the American colonies in 1752. The Gregorian calendar does not add the extra day to February in a century year unles it is divisible by four.

H

hornbook: a paddle-shaped piece of wood that colonial children used to learn to read and write.

House of Representatives: a part of congress in which the number of representatives is based on the state's population.

I

independence: the state of being separate from someone or something.

inn: a place where travelers can spend the night, eat, rest, or visit.

inoculation: a shot or medicine given to people to protect them from a certain disease or illness.

J

journal: a magazine or publication that a group or organization publishes for its members.

Julian calendar: a calendar introduced in Rome in 46 BCE. The 12-month year has 365 days except each fourth year has 366 days. Each month has 31 or 30 days, except February—which has 28 or in leap years 29 days.

Junto: the social and civic club Ben Franklin formed with his friends and other businessmen. It was also called the Leather Apron Club.

K

King George III: the king of England during the Revolutionary War.

L

Library Company of Philadelphia: the first public library that Ben Franklin and the Junto established in 1731.

lightning rod: a device that attracts lightning and carries it into the ground and away from a building, invented by Ben Franklin in 1753.

long arm: a mechanical arm invented by Ben Franklin that was used to reach books on high shelves.

loyalist: in colonial times, someone who believed America should stay under England's rule.

M

maxims: sayings or little bits of wisdom.

Minutemen: colonists who fought for independence from England.

N

New-England Courant: the newspaper Ben Franklin's brother published.

O

odometer: a device used to measure distances traveled, invented by Ben Franklin in 1785.

P

pamphlet: an informative book or brochure.

parchment: the skin of a sheep or goat prepared for writing.

Parliament: the legislative branch of the British government.

patent: a document that signifies ownership of an invention, so that no one else can get credit for it or profit from it without paying an agreed upon fee to the inventor.

Pennsylvania Assembly: the colonial government or legislature in Pennsylvania.

Pennsylvania fireplace: the fireplace insert that Ben Franklin invented in 1741.

Pennsylvania Gazette: Ben Franklin's newspaper.

Pennsylvania Hospital: America's first public hospital. Ben Franklin played a key role in getting it established in 1751.

petition: a collection of signatures, signed by a group of people, requesting that a change be made.

phonetic: spelling that reflects just how words sound.

Poor Richard's Almanac: Ben Franklin's annual almanac, published between 1732 and 1758.

postal route: traveling path a mail carrier takes to deliver the mail.

Postmaster General: an official in charge of a country's post office department.

print shop: a place where books, newspapers, and other paper and ink documents are printed.

printer: someone who prints words on paper and sells them for a living.

printing press: the machine used by printers in print shops to press ink into paper.

R

redcoats: one nickname the colonists gave the British troops.

repeal: to cancel or take back a law.

Revolutionary War: the war of independence fought between America and England between 1775 and 1783.

Richard Saunders: the fake, or pen name, Ben used to author his almanac.

riot: an out-of-control gathering of people protesting something.

rival: someone you compete against.

S

salvage sacks: bags used to collect valuables quickly during a fire before they are destroyed.

Second Continental Congress: delegates from the colonies that met to discuss whether or not America should declare its independence in 1775.

senate: a part of congress where each state is given two representatives.

separation of powers: the concept of having three different branches of government to ensure that no one branch gains more power than the others.

shilling: the money used in America during Ben Franklin's time.

Silence Dogood: the made-up name Ben Franklin signed when he wrote letters to his brother's newspaper.

smallpox: a contagious disease that killed a lot people before a vaccination for it was invented. Even though the vaccine was not perfected until 1796, after Ben Franklin died, a form of inoculation against smallpox was practiced in his time.

Stamp Act: a law England passed in 1765, requiring the colonists to buy and attach a special stamp on numerous paper goods they produced.

swim paddles: paddles someone wears on their hands to help propel them through water.

T

tavern: a place where people can buy food and drink and enjoy each other's company.

thermometer: a scientific device used to measure temperature.

treason: actions that go against one's own country.

Treaty of Alliance: an agreement from France that they would help America in its fight for independence (February 6, 1778).

Treaty of Paris 1783: an agreement between England and America that ended the Revolutionary War. With this treaty, England recognized America as a country.

tuition: the money paid to attend a privately owned school.

U

Union Fire Company: Philadelphia's first volunteer fire department. It was created by Ben Franklin in 1736.

unity: togetherness.

university: a group of colleges or a school of higher education.

University of Pennsylvania: the current name of The Philadelphia Academy and Charitable School, a boys' school established by Ben Franklin in 1751.

V

vegetarian: someone who doesn't eat meat.

virtues: positive personality traits.

W

wharf: a dock or platform built from the shore out over water.

Resources

Books

Bordessa, Kris. *Great Colonial America Projects You Can Build Yourself.* White River Junction, Vermont: Nomad Press, 2006.

Franklin, Ben. *The Autobiography of Ben Franklin.* New York, Touchstone, 2004.

Franklin, Ben (writing as Richard Saunders). *Wit and Wisdom from Poor Richard's Almanack.* New York: Dover Publications, Inc., 1999.

Fleming, Candace. *Ben Franklin's Almanac: Being a True Account of the Good Gentleman's Life.* New York: Atheneum Books for Young Readers, 2003.

Fradin, Dennis Brindell. *Who Was Ben Franklin?* New York: Grosset & Dunlap, 2002.

Isaacson, Walter. *Benjamin Franklin: An American Life.* New York: Simon & Schuster, 2003.

Kent, Deborah. *Benjamin Franklin: Extraordinary Patriot.* New York: Scholastic, 1993.

Rudy, Lisa Jo, editor. A Franklin Institute of Science Museum Book. *The Ben Franklin Book of Easy & Incredible Experiments.* New York: John Wiley & Sons, Inc., 1995.

Web sites

Autobiography of Benjamin Franklin
www.earlyamerica.com/lives/franklin/

"Benjamin Franklin"
www.postalmuseum.si.edu/exhibits/2a1c_bfranklin.html

"The Electric Ben Franklin," various articles www.ushistory.org/franklin/

"Ben Franklin Explore," various articles
www.pbs.org/benfranklin/explore.html

"Benjamin Franklin's Funeral and Grave"
www.ushistory.org/franklin/philadelphia/grave.htm

"Benjamin Franklin: Glimpses of the Man" http://fi.edu/franklin/

The Franklin Institute of Science Museum, "FAQ about Ben Franklin"
www.fi.edu/franklin/birthday/faq.html

The Liberty Bell
www.ushistory.org/libertybell/

Documentaries

Ben Franklin. Director, Joshua Alper. DVD. A&E Home Video, February 22, 2005.

Index

Image Credits